the joy experiment

by Laurence Walsh,
MA of Spiritual Psychology

15 steps from misery to joy

This book is dedicated to the stranger who gave me a wallet-sized picture of a spiritual figure and wrote on the back, "The remover of doubt will come to you soon." As an atheist for 16 years and an agnostic for 5, this was the only hope I held onto...until I relearned the truth.

Contents

Contents

introduction

> I finally figured out the only reason
> to be alive is to enjoy it.
>
> - Rita Mae Brown

CHOOSE YOU

Are you miserable?

Are you feeling stuck?

Or maybe just restless?

Do you believe you can't change?

Do you believe that where you are today is where you will always be?

The same unfulfilling relationship.

The same annoying friends.

The same hole in your heart.

The hole that you fill with alcohol, drugs, overworking, shopping, overeating, sex (if you can get it!), or too much television, if you cannot.

The hole that cannot be filled or satisfied.

A year ago, that was me.

My life was not working.

I was stressed out all the time.

Worried and frustrated.

I felt like a failure.

I was constantly sick with colds, exhaustion, and asthma. I had this broken record that played in my head all the time, "You're not good enough. You'll never do anything worthwhile. No one will ever love you." I had been fired from a prestigious television writing job on CSI: Miami; I had been dumped by my best friend of ten years; and every relationship I had ended in heartbreak.

Plus, I had migraines that would make me vomit for hours on the bathroom floor every few months. This was not the life I envisioned. This was not the life I wanted. This life was miserable.

I wanted a joyful life: one in which I look forward to work every day, share my love with a good man, and have rich, fun, supportive friendships. And a healthy, well-balanced life.

So, here's what I did:

I tried an experiment.

I set my intention to raise my levels of joy and then I took action to do it.

It wasn't easy. I had to face all my demons and set them free.

I had to recognize all the judgments I had on myself and my learned lack of value.

I had to cry and scream out all the years of repressed anger and sorrow.

I had to realize I had deeply rooted guilt about relaxing and enjoying life.

And I had to accept responsibility for making myself the victim of my own life.

But I did it.
I really did it.
I changed.
I replaced my misery with joy.
I found and cleared my old wounds.
I screamed out my early traumas.
And I gave myself the love I needed.
I replaced all my devaluing beliefs with new uplifting beliefs.

I took responsibility for my thoughts and actions.
And now I have an incredible, beautiful, joyful life.
Can you?

CHAPTER ONE:

the joy experiment

"You deserve the fun, the joy, the freedom, and the
pure goodness that flows through the experience
of love that indwells you. The choice is yours."

– David McArthur and Bruce McArthur, The Intelligent Heart

For a long time I wanted to write a book to help prevent teen
suicide. The title was "Why You Shouldn't Shoot Yourself in
the Head." It was based on my experience as a teenager
feeling trapped by depression, and also based on my
knowledge that gunshots to the head, when not successful,
are really damaging to a person's quality of life. It was only
years after I attempted to shoot myself in the head that I

discovered an incredible fact: I didn't have to feel the way I did. I could change. I didn't have to feel ugly, confused, angry, and alone. I didn't have to wallow in misery for the rest of my life. I could change those feelings by changing the underlying thoughts and emotions in my body.

"The Joy Experiment" is my final step in pushing out the old feelings and welcoming in the freedom of joy. In "The Joy Experiment," I did everything in my power to raise my levels of joy from "mediocre with clouds of gloom" to "sunshiny happiness, consistently peaceful and delighted." I made up a joy rating scale (see page 18) to measure my levels of joy throughout the day. Morning, noon, and night I filled out my joy meter (page 19) to note where I was emotionally. I checked the rating scale on how I was feeling then marked the joy meter accordingly. When I took an average over a month, I discovered I was functioning around a 5.5. I had moments of bliss, but since I was swinging into "wallowing and misery" with morning depressive jags (3s and 4s), these were averaging out to 5.5 (see my first joy meter on page 20).

On my joy rating scale, a 5 is "Just get through this. You are not your thoughts. Release judgments. Forgive others. Let go and let God. Or escape to a movie." But I want to be at an 8. An 8 is "I have a big smile on my face. My eyes are soft. I rejoice in seeing the hand of God in everyone around me. I feel safe and happy. Everything is perfect. I'm merrily singing. Love surrounds me and infuses me."

Wow, that's quite a shift in mood and perspective.

The first is tepid and scared, struggling to stay out of pain (dipping under a 5 goes into the pain zone), and the second is full of fun and excitement, enjoying every moment of this precious, sacred life.

Right now, I am declaring a moratorium on this mediocre life and setting my sites on a joyful, abundant life.

I am going to let myself be inspired and follow my intuition. Every day, I fill out a joy meter to measure my progress or digression.

Will you join me?

Check the joy rating scale to see where you are (or make up your own).

If you want, take an average over a week or a month.
This is your starting point.
Now ask yourself, "Where do I want to go?"
Dream big.
Go beyond what you can imagine.
It's an experiment after all.
You have nothing to lose.
Except that stuck, painful, boring life.
But we are going to have to be brave.
Change is a process.
It takes effort and action.
It takes focus and courage.

In order to change, you have to first admit what's not working—and that's not easy.

Sometimes we're not even consciously aware of what's not working.

Sometimes we blame ourselves for what's not working like we should magically know better.

And sometimes our body and life lashes back when we try to up-level or improve ourselves.

The hardest part in getting out of misery is being able to imagine there is something better. I hear so many people say, "my depression is chemical" and then do nothing to make a change.

Don't give up on yourself like that.

I was on anti-depressants for years staying in my unrewarding job and working crazy hours. My depression was *from my job*, but instead of treating the <u>cause</u>, I treated the <u>symptom</u>, until finally my back gave out altogether and I had to leave the job.

One reason we have pain is to tell us it's time to change. Pain says it's time to open up to new thoughts, ideas, and beliefs. It's time to let go of the old belief system that isn't supporting you. Pain encourages us to recognize what is not working in our lives and take steps to change it.

The sucky part about this Pain Feedback System is that it will keep telling you the same message louder and louder until you get it.

Take, for example, a woman whose marriage isn't working. The Pain Feedback System might first give her headaches. Then when she refuses to change or recognize what is causing the stress, it might add a car accident. Rattled, but still alive, she blames bad luck and clings to the unhealthy relationship until finally her husband leaves her for another woman, since she isn't able to get the message on her own.

As she has been in denial all along about what is for her greatest good, she will likely interpret this as a horrible event. Instead of feeling the relief that she is finally free to heal what caused the lack of love in the first place and find a supportive and loving new relationship, she will decide she is a victim and play out her life that way.

Where are you experiencing pain?
Identifying it will be the first step.

If it is in your body, that is a signal too. That says that you don't want to be aware of what is not working in your life. It's too painful to even look at—so you suppress it from awareness and it turns into acne at age 40 or extra pounds (of protection) at 50.

But healing can be easy and fun.

It is a step-by-step process.
Invest in yourself and your happiness.
Just a little time each day can make a world of difference.
Do this with me.

I am going to be honest with you.

I am going to open up and share with you my heart, my thoughts, my dreams, my desires, my secrets, my successes, and my failures. I am going to dig into my closets and pull out the pain skeletons, dust them off, take a good hard look at them and set them free.

Of course, some of this stuff could be embarrassing, but since letting go of shame is part of rising up the joy ladder, I am going to let it all hang out.

I am going to tell you where I started, what my story was, how hard I have struggled to get rid of sorrow, and how I am learning to enjoy my life.

Be brave with me.
Open up your mind to a new adventure.
Let's clear out the old junk that's keeping our lives small and see what we can create.

Honor yourself by joining me on this journey of fun…. It's your life.
You deserve it.

Some people have a negative response to words like "Love" or "God" because in the past these words have been misused. If you cringe when you read words like these or if you don't believe in "God," just substitute your own word.

Whatever means happiness to you.

"Good vibrations" or "The Force" or an aspect of nature or your favorite pet's name.

It's the same thing: Positive energy.

May the force be with you.

May the sun shine on you.

Good vibrations, man...

joy rating scale

1. Everyone is out to get me. I hate the world and it hates me. I feel like a miserable failure. Life is not worth living. Misery. Depression.

2. I feel sick. I don't want to talk to anyone. I don't want to write. I'm afraid.

3. I am alone in my little world. I've been deserted. If someone looked for me I could be found, but no one looks, no one cares. Panic.

4. Life is hard. Tomorrow is another day. You don't always get what you want in this world. Must have Island's French fries. Anxiety.

5. Just get through this. You are not your thoughts. Release judgments. Forgive others. Let go and let God. Or escape to a movie.

6. I can see the sun. The warmth feels great. I'm enjoying writing. I'm getting a lot done. I love this song. I accept my life. I'm hopeful. I am grounded in my body. Let's snuggle!

7. I have energy, drive, focus, and excitement. I feel fantastic. Life is great. Love is great. I am on the right road. I am laughing through my day. I am proud of me! I am connected to others. Doggie kisses!

8. I have a big smile on my face. My eyes are soft. I rejoice in seeing the hand of God in everyone around me. I feel safe and happy. Everything is perfect. I'm merrily singing. Love surrounds me and infuses me.

9. Yeah! Whoa! Love it! Fantastic! More! More! Yes! Thank you! I love you, God! You! Me! One! All! Ever! Forever! Love! Incredible!

DATE: _____   AVERAGE: _____

joy meter

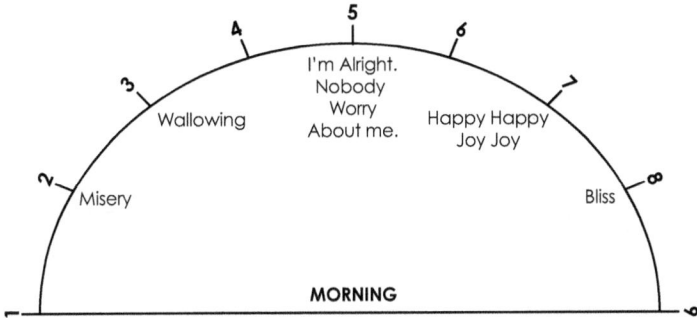

5
4   6
I'm Alright.
3   Nobody   7
Worry
Wallowing   About me.   Happy Happy
Joy Joy
2
Misery   Bliss   8

1   9

MORNING

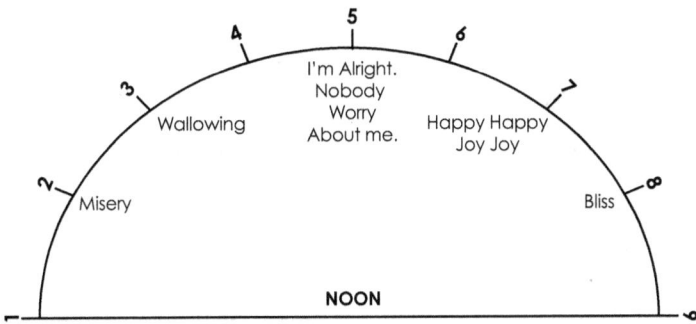

5
4   6
I'm Alright.
3   Nobody   7
Worry
Wallowing   About me.   Happy Happy
Joy Joy
2
Misery   Bliss   8

1   9

NOON

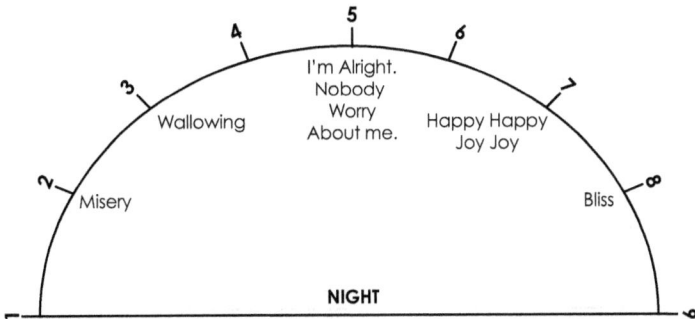

5
4   6
I'm Alright.
3   Nobody   7
Worry
Wallowing   About me.   Happy Happy
Joy Joy
2
Misery   Bliss   8

1   9

NIGHT

The Joy Experiment   19

joy meter

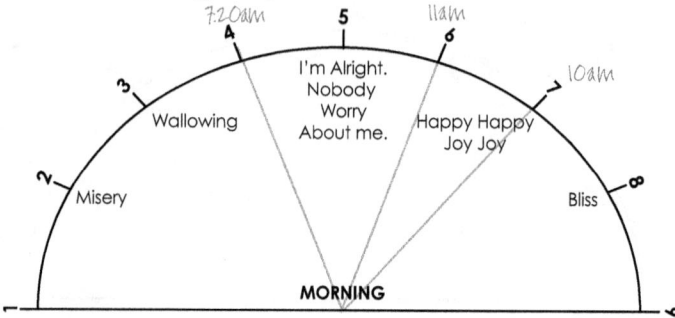

7:20am 4   **5**   11am 6   10am 7

3

Wallowing

I'm Alright. Nobody Worry About me.

Happy Happy Joy Joy

2 Misery

Bliss 8

1 **MORNING** 9

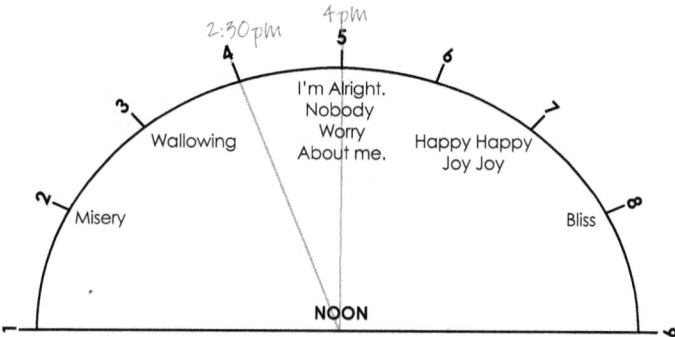

2:30pm 4   4pm **5**   6

3

Wallowing

I'm Alright. Nobody Worry About me.

Happy Happy Joy Joy

7

2 Misery

Bliss 8

1 **NOON** 9

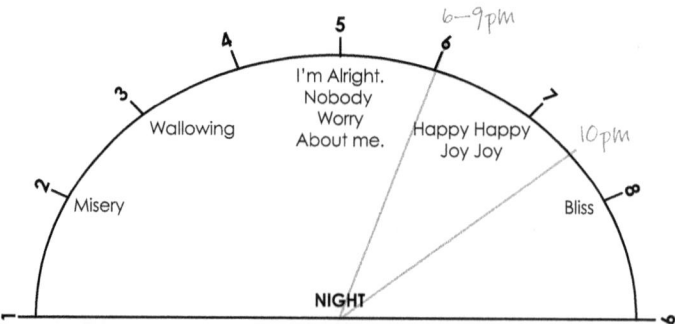

4   5   6—9pm 6   7

3

Wallowing

I'm Alright. Nobody Worry About me.

Happy Happy Joy Joy

10pm

2 Misery

Bliss 8

1 **NIGHT** 9

20   The Joy Experiment

CHAPTER TWO:

my story

"Miracles are a retelling in small letters of the very same
story which is written across the whole world in letters
too large for some of us to see."

– C.S. Lewis

The carpet in the house I grew up in was yellow shag.
I remember wearing all black. And people assumed I was an
angry teenager. Just fourteen years old.
I remember scrawling in my journal sitting on the floor of my
bedroom "I hate everyone. Everyone hates me."

I remember underlining it several times, then running down the hall—outside my body—because there was so much pain inside my body; there was no room for me.

I remember pulling the red and yellow plastic case out of the closet.

I was surprised by how heavy it was. Now, I know it was a .44. Then, I just knew it could put me out of my misery.

I picked up the magazine, checking to make sure it was chock-full of bullets. I surmised that if you shoved it in the open butt of the gun, the gun would be loaded.

I wasn't sure which way the safety latch went. So, I thought, I'll just try both ways 'til I get it right.

I put the gun into my mouth, hands shaking, tears pouring down my cheeks.

I depressed the trigger…relief was in sight… and then…

Nothing.
No Kablow.
No escape from the pain.
No, "I'll show you! I'll die!"

Frustrated, I flipped the safety to the other direction.

Now, I thought, permanent sleep. No more failure. No more embarrassment. No more pain and torture. Just sweet nothingness. I pulled the trigger.

Nothing.
Even the gun hated me.

This came as no surprise really. As someone suffering from low self-esteem, I thought, I'm a failure at committing suicide as well.

I pulled out the magazine. Took out a bullet. Put it back. Okay, so the bullets aren't glued together—that's not the problem. I put the magazine back into the gun. If Edison took 1,000 tries to make electricity, I could try shooting myself one more time.

Hands shaking, tears streaming, confusion and self-doubt setting in, I put the gun in my mouth once more.
I put my finger around the trigger and pulled.
Again. Nothing!

I threw the gun across the room screaming profanities. God damn, fuck! Shit! I'm failing Latin and I can't even kill myself right.

I put the gun neatly in its container (so as to not get into trouble for gun tampering) and retreated to my room to cry.

When I told my father about my attempted suicide, late in my thirties, his response was "Glad I never taught you to shoot."

When I told my mother I had been suicidal from the time I was 12 to the time I was 20 and had tried very seriously to kill myself at 14, her response was, "No you didn't."

But actually, I did, and I also tried to cut my wrists at least four times. Always left scars but never went very deep. And I also plotted the murder of my mother at age 13, but I will get to that…

In general, I had a good life. I was good looking, healthy and I lived in a safe neighborhood in a well-to-do upper middle class family. I had my own room. I made friends easily and loved to play witches and Barbies. I had everything a child could ask for—except love and peace of mind. Here's why…

Growing up, I loved my mother very much. I thought she was beautiful and sweet and close to God. I had two brothers that I fought with constantly. I felt that they were always hitting me or excluding me. They felt like I was always teasing them. I developed a sharp tongue at a young age. (My brother says, "You're crazy!" My response, "I'm not the one seeing a shrink!")

Anyway, I worshipped my mother and I desperately wanted "favored child status" as my older brother Preston seemed to be the hero of the family. As a matter of fact, from the age of about six, I did everything to get it, including sitting up every evening with my mother as she did the dinner dishes (avoiding going upstairs to her nightly "duties," as she called them, with my father. Cue ominous music here.)

During this time, she would tell me over and over that she wanted to kill herself, that she would be better off dead, that she had nothing to live for—"except for you kids," she sometimes added. I remember trying to argue.

I remember trying very hard to convince her that life was good, that there was a reason to live. I think at age six I identified it as "Disneyland" or "happiness." I remember insisting how much I loved her and would miss her.

But no matter how many nights I sat there and listened to her tales of woe and no matter how many times I told her "I love you, you can't die," she wanted to be dead.

Little did I know that this was not *actually* what she wanted. I found out YEARS LATER, I mean 20 years at least, that she actually just wanted attention. She needed to express her unhappiness and didn't know how to do it.

Years later, I realized that she never *actually* wanted to be dead at all. It was just something she said, like how other people say, "Money doesn't grow on trees."

But at the time, I took her threats very seriously. I constantly imagined coming home from school and seeing her hanging from the chandelier. Now that I can do the math, the chandelier would never have held her weight…

And then after years of hearing this threat, around the age of 12, I came up with the brilliant idea of putting her out of her misery.

I loved my mother so much that I wanted to be the one who gave her what she most wanted: to be embraced by a cold, deep grave. To be done and buried. All I could think of was how to kill mom. While other girls experimented with pot and kissing boys, I was obsessed with how to kill my mother.

I can't hang her—too difficult…
I can't shoot her—I'd go to jail and it's too messy…
Throwing her off a ledge would be good, but where is there a ledge high enough?
And my brothers are always with us when we hike the steep Weeping Rock in Zion.
That's when I settled on the method…
I would smother her.
Thank you, Shakespeare!

This thought made me cry. I would miss her so much after I did it. But if I really loved her, yes, I would do it. I wrote my plan out in my diary, and then I left it on the dining room table. Open. So she would read it. I can only assume she did read it because the next time I went into her room while she was sleeping to tell her the phone was for her, she sat up in bed screaming her head off in mortal terror. Oops.

The Joy Experiment

So, it was sometime after that when I decided it would be better to take myself off the earth and let her fend for herself.

It's interesting that in my adult life I spent about eight years trying to figure out how to kill people for my career. I was a procedural writer and that was my job. When I wrote on CSI: Miami and NCIS, I spent all my off hours imagining intriguing ways people could die.

They could fall off a rigged trapeze, they could be crushed with weights at the gym, or get knocked in the head in a freak wind surfing accident. Or was it an accident? I never made the correlation to my childhood until now.

Anyway, my torment went on for years. Half of the time I was a bubbly, outgoing dancer and drama student who often starred in the school play, and the other half of the time

I was depressed, lonely, and feeling betrayed by all of humanity. All through high school I thought no one in the world cared if I lived or died. Not living seemed so much better to me.

This duality went on until I was twenty, at which point I fell in love—head over heels in love with a magical, incredible man. Unfortunately, the self-hating part of me couldn't stand being so happy, so I destroyed the relationship.

In the aftermath, I realized I didn't need to live the way I was living. I didn't need to feel isolated from the world. I didn't need to be jealous of other women. I didn't need to think I was a burden to the earth. I didn't need to cry and feel horrible half the time.

I saw my given name "Melanie" in a book of definitions. It meant "darkness" or "mourner." My mom had always told me that I was a very happy child with lots of friends. I suddenly had an epiphany: Maybe I am naturally a happy, outgoing person, but I've taken on this belief system that is not mine.

My mother gave me my name and likewise gave me her "darkness" and "mourning." Under the heartbreak I felt upon losing this amazing guy, I determined I no longer wanted to feel like my life was worthless. I no longer wanted to feel I had no value. I wanted to create value and worth.
I wanted to be happy.

That's where the change started.
In my twenties, with my heart so broken that I couldn't eat,
I was determined to make a change. So,
I started with my name.
After great thought and much searching I changed my name to "Laurence."

At one point, I considered "India" but that meant "keeper of sheep," and while that's certainly better than "mourner," it wasn't exactly what I was aiming for.

"Laurence" means achievement or accomplishment.
To me it means worth.

Worth being alive.
Worth being happy.
Worth being, period.

Then I set about changing my crazy, warped, negative point of view. I could tell it was warped because my older brother acted as if he thought that he was "God." He was perfect. He even had a shirt that said, "I am God." Somehow he removed himself enough to miss the whole "I am worthless" training that I received. (Thanks Karma!)

I could see that under the same stress, he took the high road. Now, I believe both of our points of view were delusional because they were both about the ego, but if you have to have a point of view about yourself, how much better is "I am God" than "I am worthless." A lot better. Or so it seemed to me.

So, I decided to change my point of view. I stopped criticizing myself. I stopped putting myself down. I wouldn't allow even the slightest insult. Maybe because of my early ballet lessons, I have always had excellent self-discipline.

So, every time I had a negative thought about myself: that person hates me, I didn't get the acting role I wanted, I suck, I'm a failure, no boy will ever like me—I would banish the thought from my brain.

I had a lot of criticism about my looks as well. I was actually a beautiful girl, but I never allowed myself to enjoy it. Something was always wrong with me. I can't tell you how much better it is to enjoy my looks nowadays.

Now I relish every time someone calls me pretty or beautiful. Now, I am grateful for each compliment. Then, I thought people were crazy or wanted something from me (as in, he wants to get into my pants).

I read Lousie Hay's "You Can Heal Your Life." I read it over and over and over and over. I read it for years. It is about the power of positive thinking and self-love. But I was so removed from self-love that it took me sixteen years to feel it, even though I was fully committed to the path. I was 36 when I learned how to love myself.

Which brings me to the purpose of this book. I have been committed to self-love and healing for eighteen years now. I've made huge strides and tried everything along the way to heal myself.

But I can FEEL that there is something holding me back from being completely joyful. I can feel it like being in a prison or carrying a heavy weight. I need to punch through it, dissolve it, figure out what it is and chuck it in the garbage.

JOY WARNING: What I am noticing is that the more I stretch and grow in love and happiness, the more my negative thought patterns rise in resistance to being happy.

But I am committed to being fully happy. Not moderately okay. I want to enjoy each day, live life to the fullest, connect to every person I meet, trust that the man I love loves me.

I want JOY freedom.

I don't want to worry that when something good happens, something bad will happen soon shortly thereafter, or that if I love someone, I will lose them. I am ready to be fully happy. Ecstatic. Grateful. Embracing life.

But, to be honest, there is still a nudgy little voice that undermines me at moments and leaves me crying in bed wishing for an early end to it all.

Intermittently, that voice says, "You can't write a book. Everyone will make fun of you. Who would want to read it?" But I'm going to show you, voice of low self-esteem! You can't stop me! I can out-create you!

So, that's where I came from. Let's see where I'm headed: I want to embrace joy. I want to take my current spotty, inconsistent, externally-created joy and transform it into blissful, inner-created, overflowing ecstasy.

Come with me!!

Let's start off by setting our intentions…

The Joy Experiment

CHAPTER THREE:

setting intentions and visualizing possibilities

Intentions and Visualizations are powerful ways to set up and reach a goal. They can also act as a subconscious guide to help us manifest our dreams.

MY JOY INTENTIONS:
It is my intention to love myself no matter what is going on in my life.
It is my intention to feel bliss in my body.
It is my intention to be full of gratitude for the beautiful abundance in my life.

It is my intention to unconditionally accept all aspects of myself.

It is my intention to enjoy my life.

It is my intention to trust love.

It is my intention to manifest a soulmate.

It is my intention to open my heart.

It is my intention to trust God to support me completely.

It is my intention to be grateful to God.

It is my intention to spread joy and excitement to others.

It is my intention to appreciate what I have been given.

It is my intention to fully embrace all that life offers me.

It is my intention to face my fears and let go of them.

It is my intention to live deeply and fully.

It is my intention to love life.

It is my intention to love myself and others.

It is my intention to take a vacation.

What are your intentions?

I encourage you to set some right now.

Intentions give our lives purpose and action. They act as a guide to what we want to create. Try it. It's easy. They can be anything. For example, I intend to make a boatload of money or I intend to smile at more people. You can always add more as the ideas come to you. What would you like in your life? Go big. Don't be shy. Intend it.

It is my intention to _____

_____.

It is my intention to_____

_____.

It is my intention to _____

_____.

It is my intention to _____

_____.

It is my intention to _____

_____.

It is my intention to _____

_____.

It is my intention to _____

_____.

It is my intention to _____

_____.

It is my intention to _____

_____.

It is my intention to _____

_____.

It is my intention to _____

_____.

It is my intention to _____

_____.

It is my intention to _____

_____.

It is my intention to _____

_____.

It is my intention to _____

_____.

visualizing the possibilities

"I can't believe that!" said Alice.
"Can't you?" the Queen said in a pitying tone.
"Try again: draw a long breath, and shut your eyes."
Alice laughed. "There's no use trying."
She said: "One can't believe impossible things."
"I daresay you haven't had much practice," said the
Queen. "When I was your age, I always did it for half-
an-hour a day. Why, sometimes I've believed as many
as six impossible things before breakfast."

- Alice in Wonderland by Lewis Carroll

What would a joyful Laurence be like?
Relaxed. Open. Affectionate. Self-expressive. Joyful.
This Laurence would jump out of bed knowing she was
creating wonderful stories for the world.
I would be confident that I am on the right path, fulfilling my
life's purpose.

I would be co-creating my life with spirit and therefore have an inner knowing that everything that happens is perfect.
I would be unshakable in my loving and self-appreciation.
I would be accepting great abundance into my life.
I would be making love with my soulmate and creating a beautiful life with him.
I would be celebrating myself, my family, and my friends.
I would be peaceful in my heart and mind.
I would be giving love to myself and others.
I would have incredible health, beauty, and radiance.
I would be in the flow of life.
I would be taking time to relax and rejuvenate.
I would be connected to God through gratitude.
All my needs would be met before I even asked.
I would be emanating love wherever I go.
I would be vibrating with excitement for life.

Can you picture your perfect life?
What would you be like?
What could you feel like?
Can you imagine knowing your life purpose?
Can you imagine cherishing yourself and your relationships?
Can you imagine an easy, graceful flowing life?
Try right now…let there be no limits.

No one is going to see this or grade this or criticize this.
If you're not in the mood or can't think of anything good, just imagine having peace of mind or strength of heart to get through this trying time.

But the more you can let go of the "pain story" and imagine what you want your story to be, the closer you will get.
Just take a deep breath, relax your body, and write down what you want your life to be.
The movie version if you will.
Don't hold back.
Include Bradley Cooper.

_____

_____

_____

_____

_____

_____

_____

_____

_____

_____

_____

The Joy Experiment

CHAPTER FOUR:

where am i now with joy?

**"Sometimes it is harder to deprive oneself
of a pain than of a pleasure."**

– F. Scott Fitzgerald

I'm all over the map.

I'm ecstatically in love.

I'm on the bathroom floor vomiting with a migraine.

I'm joyfully walking with my good friend Katrina.

I'm curled up in a ball crying on my bed thinking I'll never get another writing job again.

I'm dancing my heart out at my ecstatic dance class.

I'm having another conversation about my fears with my boyfriend.

I'm broken up with said boyfriend.

I am proud of myself for finishing a script.

I am waking up in the middle of the night in a cold sweat from a nightmare.

I am laughing and making silly faces with my nephew JJ.

I am in the tub sobbing, thinking about slitting my wrists.

I am loving eating shabu hachi in Pasadena.

Okay, I'm a little uneven.

All my joy comes from the outside right now.

I do something to get happy.

I talk to someone.

I go dancing.

I read a joyful book.

I get a massage. Yummy!

I see a movie, a million movies. (Well, that's part of my job).

But I want that joy to come from within me no matter what.

I want to be the JOY GENERATOR!

Now let me remind you where I was with joy and then you'll see I've actually come a long way already:

Ever since I was six, I've had these crying jags. Back then, I had an enormous stuffed whale called Whaley that I would hug as I cried myself to sleep. I would cry really loud to try to get someone's attention, but that never worked. I don't even remember what I was crying for. Yes, I wanted attention. Yes, I was afraid of being possessed by the devil. But wasn't every kid? And yes, my mother was horribly depressed and told me about it in detail.

In my twenties, when I decided not to be sad anymore, I still spent hours on end crying. At first, I got very good at doing other things as I cried. I could do an entire step workout with Jane Fonda while tears rolled down my face. I could read hours of Philosophy homework, -- though the books got pretty wet.

Then I found anti-depressants, which stopped the crying for a while and gave me some lovely feelings of self-esteem (even if they weren't real or lasting). But I didn't want to be on medication for the rest of my life. And, as I said, pain exists to show us where we need to change. So, after about five years of being buoyed by Prozac and Wellbutrin, I stopped taking anti-depressants and started doing the actual healing work.

During this time, I was in therapy, but I still had crying jags that would last anywhere between ten minutes and two hours. They are sometimes correlated to a subject "I don't have a job—waaaa!" or "I want my boyfriend to pay more attention to me—waaa!"

But through the "The Joy Experiment," I kept track of my feelings in a patterning journal and discovered something incredible. The cause of my tears was exchangeable.

The moment I resolved one issue, another <u>identical</u> issue conveniently stepped in to take its place. So either the crying came for no reason or the reason itself changed.

Which lead me to an important revelation:

What I think is upsetting me isn't what's upsetting me.

It looks real.

It feels real.

It comes in the order of cause and effect.

But if I look deeper, I would have the effect—the crying—anyway.

So, I might as well stop blaming the supposed "cause."

Last month the "causes" were:

I don't get enough attention from my boyfriend.

I don't have a job.

I'm afraid I love my boyfriend more than he loves me.

Earlier this year the "causes" were:

I'm 38 and I'm not married.

I don't have my own family.

I'm not normal.

I'll never get hired as a writer.

Before that the "causes" were:

A director has hijacked my film.

My ex-best friend ripped me off $60,000.

My mother is seriously depressed and drives me nuts.

You can see how the negative thoughts just replace each other.

Try keeping a journal.

Even if you write only 1 page a day.

You will see the same thing.

Once you clear up one issue, the same issue rears its head in a different form.

Why is that?

Why is my life playing a broken Doo-wop record of rejection?

Because these "causes" are trying to get me to clear THE TRAUMAS FROM MY PAST.

I believe these traumas are the reason I continue to sob uncontrollably.

The reason I haven't had an enduring relationship.

The reason "friends" keep betraying me.

The people and events are ONLY a mirror to my inner reality.

As a child, I interpreted my mother as rejecting me, and then I formed a misbelief in my mind that I was not worthy of love, and then those misbeliefs replay and replay to get me to do the work to get rid of the false belief.

That is why I continue to have the same issues in relationships over and over.

I have a wound that needs healing and until I heal it, I will continue to replay the original trauma.

Once was bad enough, but over and over again for 38 years?

You might be wondering at this point where those misinterpretations came from?

It's a guessing game of a child's memory.
This is not about blaming the parents.
They were doing the best they could.
Aren't we all?

Psychologist Ron Hulnick's favorite saying is "Most people don't wake up think, 'How can I fuck up my child today?'"
This is about clearing the false beliefs I CREATED when I was a child.

There is only one solution now.
First, I need to cry out all the tears.
Then, I need to change those underlying dastardly beliefs that I made up to explain what happened.
Finally, I need to reset my inner comfort levels to love, peacefulness and joy.
And this is all so I can be happy.
Really happy.
Writing this book, I am uncovering those past traumas and working to heal them.
I know that in the past, I abandoned myself.
I gave up on myself.
I got this idea that other people's lives were better and more important than mine.
There are some roots of those old feelings of worthlessness still planted beneath my feet.
And I am responsible for getting them out!

In the same way, I am responsible for planting the new roots of self-nurturing and love.

Every time I feel bad, you can bet it is from a negative thought that got planted in my subconscious from some mistaken belief I created!

Then that mistaken belief plays out on the stage of my life begging me to let go of it.

It's like the child whose parents divorce and the child thinks it's his fault. Of course, it had nothing to do with the child. Chances are, the child was actually holding the marriage together, but when the parents split, the child gets it in his head, "There's something wrong with me. I made Dad leave."

Then as the child grows up, over and over again, people leave. He loses his faith in love and that becomes his reality. Until the pain becomes so great that he finally decides to do some healing work. He chooses to look into his uncleared traumas and figure out what false conclusions he created.

Sometimes our anger and hatred is so great. Our feelings of betrayal are so profound that we can't get past them. We can't take responsibility for where we are in life. We can't even see the repeated pattern.

That is why being aware of your patterns is so important. If you can see how you replay a relationship over and over, then you can stop blaming the people involved. You can ride that feeling back to the earliest time you felt it and you can discover the false belief that created the pattern.

A human being's true nature is love. When we have false beliefs about ourselves, it's difficult to feel our true nature.

So, to recap:

I am causing these 'broken record' events in my life so I can continue to replay my earliest traumas. So I can cry and be miserable.

I am the reason I don't have a job.

I am the reason I don't have a boyfriend.

Those "causes" are trying desperately to get me to look at my UNDERLYING BELIEFS.

Of course, I don't want to because the underlying beliefs SUCK!

They hurt.

Bringing them up makes me afraid.

But yet, they are there.

Regardless of how they got there.

My underlying beliefs are not going to disappear because I pretend they are not there!!!!!

And I am committed to getting rid of them.

These false beliefs are the reason my joy meter slides into wallowing. They are the reason I am not bubbling over with self-confidence and love.

Before I tell you how I am going to get rid of my false beliefs,
I want to check in with you.
What is playing on your broken record?
What was the message your mom or dad repeated to you as
a child?
"You'll never amount to anything!"
Or the sad, repetitive message, "life is a struggle"... "and
then you die."

If you don't know your broken record off hand, try this:
Find a place to be alone.
Sit quietly with your eyes closed.
Focus on your breath coming in and going out.
And now feel.
What do you feel in your body?
What thoughts float into your head?
Use the following page to jot down things that are causing
you pain or have caused you pain in the past.
Jot down areas of your life that need fixing.
Jot down the names of people who slighted you or people
you hate.
These people will be your ROAD MAP to your early trauma.
Don't get overwhelmed.
We're going to go step by step.
Healing takes time.
And you'll be happy you did it!

_____

_____

The Joy Experiment

_____

_____

_____

_____

_____

_____

_____

_____

_____

_____

_____

_____

_____

_____

_____

_____

The Joy Experiment

clearing out the old traumas

"The only thing to fear is fear itself."

– Franklin D. Roosevelt

At first, I tried to raise my joy levels by doing fun stuff like getting massages and hanging out with friends more regularly, but it became readily apparent that that wasn't where the focus was needed. This was an inside job. That is, I needed to change how I felt about things, not the things themselves. To do that, I needed to go inside and examine my thoughts, beliefs, and emotions. Without changing those, the world just wasn't going to look bright and shiny and magical like I was intending.

Unless you've done major healing work clearing your childhood traumas, then all of your unprocessed emotions are sitting in your body clogging up your fun.

All of that anger and sadness you refused to feel in grade school, high school, college, on the job, in your marriage, or in your divorce are clogging up your heart like plaque on an artery. You cannot feel your natural joy of life with all these old pains in the way.

Also, if you don't process your feelings, you run the risk of projecting them onto someone else or having someone close to you express them for you.

The only way to get to the joy is to heal the traumas. There are a few things that make it challenging to clear out the old traumas: suppression of feelings, denial of feelings, and the process of feeling the feelings and expressing them.

The first challenge to expressing one's feelings is that many people choose to suppress their feelings rather than express them. They do this through addictions: overeating, sex, drugs, drinking, or co-dependence.

Addictions are a misguided effort to maximize pleasure and minimize pain. But all they actually do is create a false pleasure and end up forestalling pain. People who suppress feelings through addictions don't realize that they are just delaying the emotions they are going to have to face eventually (unless they kill themselves with their addiction).

And, they are creating more pain on top of what they are suppressing through guilt, self-loathing, and the physical damage the addiction does.

The second challenge to clearing the old traumas is that many people are in denial of their feelings. Therefore, they can't get in touch with them in order to release them. This is because we live in a world where it is not okay to have feelings. We're not used to safely expressing anger and sorrow. Especially without someone or something to blame.

In order to not be rejected, we suppress our feelings, which again, doubles the pain. When we don't express our feelings, we cut off from our emotions. We deaden ourselves to everything. But our emotions are there and they are determined to be felt, so they show up as sickness, or in projections onto other people, or in "overreactions."

It seems like the only acceptable way to have feelings in America today is to feel them through television and film characters. That doctor on "House" is such an ass, but I'm sure we'd all like to speak our minds, tell everyone off, and have the last word.

All our tears and joy are one step removed. It's okay to cry in movies but not in real life? Our culture is obsessed with productivity and doesn't give people room to be human, to simply BE. One needs to be still and quiet to feel their feelings. Then, one needs to be brave to express their sorrow, regret, and frustration. If you feel nothing right now, rest assured…you have feelings and you can reach them.

The third challenge is actually feeling the feelings in order to process them and set them free. And those dark, suppressed feelings can feel scary. For one, they are years old. You probably won't even recognize them. The trauma and misbeliefs could be from something that happened in the womb, or at age 2, 4, 8, or 16. So, the mind can't make rational sense of them. Also, the feelings can cover the whole range of negative emotions: terror, discomfort, hatred, guilt, desire, desperation, shame, humiliation, confusion and even some positive feelings are suppressed like desire.

Letting them come up when they are unattached to a "cause" or origin can feel disorienting. Letting intense feelings of hatred come up at all is against everything we've been taught as a good member of society.

But that is how I got healthy and happy. I had to fully express my intense hatred of my mother (not to her) and then let it go. Being with intense feelings as they pass through your body can feel like you are losing your mind. But it is worth facing them to get rid of the constant underlying anxiety or complete numbness you can feel when you don't process your feelings.

Right now, if you are not abundantly happy, it's because you have uncleared traumas. I realized this because as I was trying to raise my level of joy, I kept hitting pain and sorrow. The more I clear the sorrow, the more I feel the joy.

PAIN IS A GREAT MOTIVATOR ON THE SPIRITUAL PATH. PAIN FORCES US TO CHANGE, TO SOFTEN, TO FORGIVE, TO LET GO OF PERCEIVED WRONGS.
I WOULD NEVER BE THIS CLOSE TO GOD IF I HADN'T HAD SO MUCH PAIN TO CLEAR.

The first step is to cry out all the tears.
Since I've been crying from the time I was 6 to 38, you'd think I'd be done. You'd think I'd cried it all out.

But most of that time was spent REHASHING the same old trauma. RELIVING the victim story that I didn't have a mother or father, that I was verbally abused by my mother's suicide threats, that I was alone in the world, that I was abandoned by God, and that I would be left by anyone I loved. That is the BROKEN RECORD I told myself over and over again to justify why my life was the way it was.
What I needed to do was HEAL the original trauma. Cry the tears for that memory. Then recognize the false thoughts I created and change the underlying beliefs. (I will talk about how to change the underlying beliefs in chapter 6.)

IT'S A TWO-STEP PROCESS:
      1.   Feel the grief and pain of the original trauma

2.   Change the limiting belief that was created at
the time of the trauma.

FEELING THE FEELINGS

Many people can't even tell you how they are feeling. They
are unaware of what bothers them, what triggers the need to
have another glass of wine, what triggers the underlying
anxiety that dampens their mood daily. They can't figure out
why they feel stuck or why life feels unsatisfying.

In order to get back in touch with those childlike feelings of
joy, we need a METHOD to clear the underlying, hidden
feelings that we've been suppressing all our lives. Some
people do kick-boxing, some meditate, some yell at their
family and friends (not recommended), but I've found he
most powerful and effective way to clear negative feelings
from the past is called Pranayama Yoga Breathing. The
specific version that I practice was developed by a talented
clairaudient healer named David Elliott.

The breathwork allows you to face your fears and process
them. No more repressed sorrow rising up as anxiety. I did
this meditation every day for a year.

PRANAYAMA YOGA BREATHING –
Is an ancient breathing meditation that uses a double breath, first
into the belly and then into the chest. This style of breathing
oxygenates the cells, stimulates the amygdala to release old fears,
and stimulates the hypothalamus to secret endorphins. The
collective effect detoxifies the mind, body, and spirit and returns
the breather to their natural state, which is joy.

I've been doing this breathwork for around a half hour a day for over two years. When I started doing this meditation, I used to scream bloody murder. I had so much suppressed negative energy to release. I had to scream out the anger out so I could get to the tears. Then I would cry bloody murder. I felt like I would die just laying on a bed breathing. I felt like creepy demons possessed my body. I felt like I was facing every negative thought I ever had about myself. All my anger at my parents. All the resentments for every lost relationship, every lost friend, every lost job—plus all the anger and sorrow I had because I judged myself for having so much anger and sorrow! Then I would release the fears from my body. I sent them up to the dark side of the moon to be dissolved into the nothingness from which they came.

The more I released, the better and lighter I felt. The happier I became. Then, after months and months of releasing pent up emotions, the crying stopped. The major traumas were cleared. Now when I meditate, smaller judgments might come into my awareness and a few tears might trickle down my cheeks as I release those misunderstandings. In the beginning, I was grieving for my lost childhood; now I am clearing up smaller negative feelings that might take the thought form, "Why didn't that guy call me?" This thought form immediately makes me feel bad in my body. When I meditate and release it through the breath, I discover the underlying belief, "Something is wrong with me and therefore he doesn't love me." I continue to breathe and release tension that rises up in my body, and I discover, once again, that old misbelief: "I am unlovable."

Now that the pain is released, the breath brings in glorious vibrations and loving energy. I feel myself naturally filling up with positive feelings and I am able to rewrite the old painful belief into a healthier and more realistic belief: "It has nothing to do with me that he didn't call. That is his choice. I am completely lovable and some man will love me completely." (A year later as I am editing this book, even those misunderstandings have disappeared.)

My website www.joyinfinite.com offers numerous meditations that can guide you to Self-Love, Forgiveness, Self-Esteem, and much, much more!

THE BREATHWORK

Here is the process:
First, find a private place where you can be alone.
Then, lie down on the bed or floor (with a yoga mat or carpet) with nothing under your head.
Relax your body and let thought drifts out of your mind.

Set your intention for the breath session.
For example, "My intention is to clear any negative energy that can be cleared at this time" or "I want to release feelings of unworthiness for the last time."

Close your eyelids. Use an eye pillow if that is easier.

Inhale through your mouth into your stomach letting it expand like a balloon.
Then, without exhaling, take a second breath into your chest, letting your rib cage and the area around your heart expand. Then exhale all through your mouth.

Each step should take one second. Inhale, inhale, exhale. You should be able to hear your breath: in, in, out. You should be able to feel your stomach rise, your breasts or pecs rise and then fall.

Allow your hands to rest at your sides.
People have different sensations when they start breathing. The more you relax, the better.

For newbies, resistance can rise immediately.
Your ego wants to keep you where you are. It doesn't want to release the pain. It wants to maintain the status quo. The ego is the voice telling you that you can't change. It is the voice telling you that you'll never be happy. The ego is the voice that doesn't believe meditation is cool.

Resistance can take the form of thinking you are hyperventilating. It can take the form of a sudden headache. It can take the form of your hand squeezing into tight angry balls. Or feeling like you are going to freeze to death. These thoughts are trying to rationalize the feelings as they arise. Your ego is trying to hold on to the negative energy. Just let the feelings come up. Let go of control for this short time.

And keep breathing.

The breath gets your blood circulating and takes you out of your head.

Breathe into any area that hurts. Let the breath surround and clear those places.

Usually people will start to feel tingling in their face and hands. This happens when the cells start to finally get new oxygen. The good energy begins to move into the cells and release the bad.

At this point, David Elliott recommends people say aloud: "It is safe to be in my body." This allows us to be really present to our body and feelings. Otherwise, we might dissociate or go elsewhere in an effort to once again avoid the pain. You can also say "It is safe to feel my feelings."

Each breath session is different. I usually ask people to begin with a scream. I ask them to scream as loud and as long as possible.

It is amazing to me how hard it is for people to really scream. The scream does several things. It tells your body that you are open to expressing your feelings. For people who have not felt their feelings in a long time, it begins the powerful process of connecting them to underlying suppressed feelings of anger that are so taboo in Western society. And finally, my experience is that the anger must be released before the sorrow can be reached.

Over and over again, I've seen the layers peel away like this:

ANXIETY
NUMBNESS/ FRUSTRATION/ IRRITATION
ANGER
SORROW
GRIEF/ TRAUMA
NEUTRALITY
HAPPINESS
JOY
LAUGHTER
BLISS

If you are having trouble reaching a feeling state it could be because you haven't taken responsibility for yourself and your life. If you blame your husband for your pain, then your mind will not allow your body to clear the pain. It happens like magic: the moment I take responsibility for whatever happened (from a clerk being rude to me to my mother telling me that kids are a lot of trouble and not really worth it), the underlying feelings are freed.

After you scream, keep breathing.

If you feel tightness, scream again, or let out a big fake laugh.

This laugh lightens the process and frees us from taking "healing" too seriously.

These feelings aren't you. The anger you feel toward your parents is a misunderstanding. You have anger inside of you that needed an outlet. It's part of being human. Don't identify with the anger or sorrow as it leaves—just let it go.

This is what Eckhart Tolle calls the pain body. We are all born with it and in life we can either add to it (by believing the lies that people don't love us or we are not good enough) or we can process our feelings, set the pain body free, and enjoy our bodies and our lives.
Still breathing…

After the amygdala (an almond-shaped mass of matter deep inside the brain) releases the stored trauma and the fear is released, the endorphins from the hypothalamus will start to kick in and feelings of elation will occur.

You can do the breathwork for five minutes or for a half hour. I usually measure my breath session by how I feel. I breathe until any negativity or feelings of being afraid are replaced by feelings of being loved and held, and I'm feeling optimistic about my future. I also wait until I receive a message about what my next step that day is, such as…"write this scene" or "email so-and-so" or "go for a walk."

ENERGY WARNING! Occasionally, it becomes apparent that what you are feeling is someone else's energy. Here is a very powerful way to clear that energy, which was taught to me by chiropractor Dr. Susan Benedict.

The Joy Experiment

*First, say out loud or in your head that you give them back their
energy and take your energy back from them. Next, visualize
cutting all ties, bonds, promises or "cords" with that person.
Visualize pulling out any hooks that were in you where the cords
connected and bury them deeply in the earth. Allow them to melt
back into molten lava.*

*Visualize white light healing all the places where the hooks came
into you until the wounds are healed and you are whole and
complete again.*

*This powerful clearing can be effective immediately or may need
to be repeated. You will feel a distinct difference when you clear
someone's energy from your body.*

Once you have processed and released your feelings, now it
is time to refuel. You have just cleared the negative energy
out of your body so it feels wonderful to refill with positive
energy. Now, transition from two breaths to one deep breath.
Sometimes I use guided visualizations at this point. I hold my
inner child lovingly or I visualize my breath swirling inside my
body caressing each organ and cell.

If you want, you can imagine someone who loves you
unconditionally putting their hand on your heart. This is a
great way to allow the love to fill every space in your body. I
have also experienced a number of visions at this point in
the meditation. I once saw a very slow turtle crawling up my
body and into my heart. I felt the turtle anchoring in my deep
self-loving. Another time, I saw a thunderbird (American
Indian totum for unlimited happiness) spread its wings
magnificently above me. At the same time, a breather next to

me was blessed with a visit from her deceased Grandmother out in their favorite lavender field.

What is important is to let the light in. Let it fill your body and be energized by it. Often people will spontaneously laugh at this point because they feel so joyful.

This deep breath carries light and love into the spaces you've opened from the two-part breath. After at least ten minutes of relaxed breathing, I recommend acknowledging yourself for the great work you did. You can be proud of yourself for taking time to love yourself. You can acknowledge yourself for raising your vibration and co-creating the life you want.

This is a good time to put your hands over your heart and feel the vibrant energy of love you have within you. Or if a part of your body is still contracting, you can put your hands and attention on this part and breath the opening, healing breath there. This part can last from ten minutes to an hour, depending on how much time you need to re-energize.

Finally, to come back into your body, you can wiggle your toes, roll your ankles, shake your hands, wiggle your hips, stretch your arms above your head, move your head from side to side, take off the eye mask, and open your eyes.

Then roll to your side and slowly push yourself up, taking as much time as you need.

Great job! You are amazing! Can you feel the joy? Free. Plentiful. And at your fingertips.

BREATHWORK WARNING! If at any time the pain or fear feels overwhelming, stop the breath and find a David Elliott certified Pranayama Breathwork practitioner in your area.

Note your experience here:

_____

_____

_____

_____

_____

_____

_____

_____

_____

_____

The Joy Experiment

CHAPTER SIX:

getting rid of old belief systems

"**An old belief is like an old shoe. We so value its comfort that we fail to notice the hole in it.**"

– Robert Brault

How many minutes or seconds can you go without a negative thought? I'm going to time myself right now and see how many minutes I can go.

It's 1:09 right now.

At 1:45pm, I had a negative thought.

That was 36 minutes.

It used to be that I couldn't go 3 minutes without my mind wandering to some self-criticism or judgment of someone else.

(As I edit this, I can go 24 hours without a negative thought.) These negative thoughts served a purpose when we were kids; they protected us from getting hurt. But as adults, most of our negative thinking just holds us back from going after what we want and living true to ourselves.

Usually these voices are not even ours. Usually you can identify a parent or grandparent or teacher who repeated this message to you. This message that you picked up and believed to be your own.

When you do the Pranayama Yoga breathing, it can tap into the underlying grief and bring up all these old issues.

My issues used to be:
"I am worthless."
"I am unlovable."
"No man will ever love me."
"Anyone I love will leave me."
But they never showed up as those statements. They showed up as: "Why would I want to go out with that guy. He's not good enough for me." Or, "I feel alienated from my fellow writers."

The real underlying beliefs were deeply buried in my subconscious and I had to pull them out to clear them.

I had to process all the pain associated with these feelings and then rewrite the inner dialogue in my brain.

"My thoughts and opinions are valuable."

"I am lovable."

"My soulmate loves me."

"Love lasts."

Unless you change the core belief, you will continue to be haunted by these repeating thoughts and they will continue to manifest in reality in different ways, such as your lover, boyfriend, girlfriend, wife, husband not treating you right or leaving in order to reinforce your underlying belief.

How could they!

Those meanies.

If you have a victim story,
If you say, "I'm upset because...",
If you say, "Why does this always happen to me?"
You have an underlying false belief.

So, how do we figure out the truth of the situation? How do I transition from an underlying subconscious belief that I am unlovable to a new conscious belief that is 100% true—that I am lovable?

My psychology teacher would say that everything is love and that which is not love is not true.

So, if we let go of the false beliefs, we will be in love.

But, in case you have a hard time believing that, think about it this way:

As I have changed my core beliefs about people, people have changed their behavior towards me.

Last year, I had a projection that my sister and I weren't as close as we used to be. I was bemoaning it until I decided to look at the belief that I had that was creating it. I lay down for a breath session and traced the feeling back to its origin, cleared up the original misunderstanding, and came to a peaceful place with our relationship. My sister called five minutes later to tell me about her life.

Another time, I breathed through my belief that my older brother excluded me from family gatherings. I traced the feeling back to the first times I felt excluded, when I was an angry teenager who hated everyone and thought everyone hated me. I cleared up this root misperception (that I was unwanted and unloved) and replaced it with a more beneficial belief system: people like me. My brother called the following day to invite me for a week's vacation at Disneyworld. It seems like a miracle, but it is simply removing the negative energy that was blocking him from including me and shifting it to accepting energy—and all the way in Pittsburgh, he felt the shift and called.

ENERGY WARNING! This isn't to say that you don't also need to address issues with other people, creating boundaries or asking for what you want. But I do suggest you clear the energy around

The Joy Experiment

an issue within yourself first. Then if the situation doesn't shift by itself, it may be time to speak your truth.

Your energy creates your experiences.

I have a writing friend who has victim energy from his upbringing. He got mugged twice in 36 hours while on vacation and is continually the butt of jokes at parties. It may seem like people are picking on him, but I believe his energy is attracting the gibes. If he cleared the underlying beliefs, the comments and mistreatment would stop.

People do what you believe they will do.
If you think your son or daughter won't love you, they won't love you. Because that is what you are creating.
Your perspective shapes what you see in the world.

So, would you rather have people be kind to you, love you, hire you, choose you, pay attention to you, and respect you? Or would you rather have people treat you poorly, dump you, betray you, make fun of you, and disrespect you?

The choice is yours.
All you have to do is change your negative underlying beliefs.
I know, that sounds challenging. And it can be.

But consider the alternative:

Living an unhappy life, frustrated with people treating you badly.

It's at least worth a try.
I am going to give you several different methods for uncovering the subconscious beliefs so that you can change your life.

First, how can you recognize an old belief pattern?
Here is an easy test: If a thought comes from fear, it's part of the old pattern.
If it comes from love, it is the truth.
Here is another test: If a thought makes you feel bad in your body, it probably comes from fear.
If it feels good (and doesn't hurt anyone), it comes from love.

The reason I put the caveat above is that sometimes people get their love and pain wires crossed if they grow up associating love with pain.

I am currently in a Master's program in Spiritual Psychology where they teach all the methods of changing the subconscious limiting beliefs. These methods are based on leading psychological techniques tested and found successful for identifying and releasing limiting beliefs.

GET HELP
Also, if at any point you feel overwhelmed by the emotions or fears brought up, GET HELP. Call a therapist. Call the suicide hotline (I did, three times!). Call a friend. Call anyone. Change can

be very challenging. The issues arising can be very painful. You don't have to go through the process alone. There are so many support groups: AA, OA, MA, NA. Alanon. Book club. Sometimes releasing issues can also release toxins in your body since you are changing on a cellular level. I support myself by taking salt baths, getting massages, seeing a non-force chiropractor, and visiting an energy healer who clears negative energy.Take time to go inside and ask yourself what support you need to make these changes.

Here are a few different methods for uncovering the subconscious beliefs:

GIVE THE ISSUE/PROBLEM/PAIN A VOICE

This is such a fantastic way to honor yourself. When something hurts, it is because you are out of balance. The pain is a guide telling you where you need to correct. Like a hangover after drinking. It is a clear message that the amount that was consumed was too much for the body. It created too many toxins for the body to handle and now the body feels ill. Likewise, any pain or problem has a message for us. Sometimes we avoid the pain with painkillers because we are afraid of the message.

Here is an example of me giving my clogged nose a voice:

CLOGGED NOSE (CN): Hi.

LAURENCE (L): Hi, Clogged nose. Anything I can do for you?

CN: No, I'm fine.

L: Why do you think you are clogged?

CN: I'm sick of other people telling me what to do and you listening to that.

L: Tell me more.

CN: You never do what I want to do.

L: What do you want to do?

CN: I want to get sexy. Have fun. Play around with men.

L: Really? Why's that?

CN: Because I am deprived of fun. Your life is boring. Like a clogged nose.

L: Really? You need more excitement?

CN: I want to go out and see new sights and smell new smells.

L: But when you are clogged, I have to stay home.

CN: Even if I weren't clogged, you'd stay home.

L: You're right. I'm very comfortable at home. I love to be home and get all warm and cuddly with my boys (dogs).

CN: Well, I don't. I want to go out and have fun and shake the dust off my feet.

L: There's dust on your feet?

CN: I want romance and adventure and love.

L: I hear you.

CN: I want to travel and see the world.

L: Really?

CN: I want to meet new people and adventure around.

L: What else?

CN: I like beautiful sites and wonders.

L: I hear you.

CN: I'm tired of working my life away. Let's retire and travel.

L: That's a thought. Not sure we can pay for that.

So, now I have more insight into what is causing my illness—a lack of enjoyment in my life. Once I am aware of what is going on, I can take small steps to correct it, such as committing to take a vacation or going dancing with friends once a week. I can be aware of ways to have fun and play even while I'm working.

If you try this method, bring your kindest, most loving self forward to talk to the aspect. Sometimes the aspect can be very unruly, so in order to not get dragged into the aspect's position, it is important to use your most loving self to deal with the issues. At the school where I got my degree in Spiritual Psychology, we call this aspect your Inner Counselor. Your Inner Counselor is the wisest, most intuitive part of yourself. Your inner guru. The part of you that is beyond fear and ego and is aligned to your greatest joy and your life purpose. It is the unconditionally loving part of you. Your essence.

You can tell the difference between the voice of your ego and the voice of your Inner Counselor by examining the words or advise given. If the guidance comes from fear and is about protecting yourself, then it is the voice of your ego. If the guidance brings messages of excitement, love, or trust, it is your wise Inner Counselor.

If you struggle to hear the voice of your Inner Counselor, remember a time in your life that you felt anchored in feelings of deep love, joy and trust. Then respond to your issue from that place. (Also, chapter 10 will help!)

NON-DOMINANT HANDWRITING

This means literally putting the pen in your other hand and writing. It looks messy, but quickly connects us to our inner child. Perhaps it is because it switches functioning to the other side of your brain. For most of us right handers, guided by our logical left brain, it allows us to move into the hemisphere that holds the emotions, creativity, and a broader perspective of the whole. Author Michael Faust believes the right brain gives people "…an in-built kit for communicating with their soul."

Non-dominant handwriting also slows us down so that we have time to connect to the emotions that the aspect is experiencing. If you allow the inner aspect to speak freely—unjudged, unedited, and uncensored—you could learn a lot about yourself and what you need to be happy.

FREE-FORM WRITING

This is the process of putting a pen to paper and expressing what you are feeling. Often times, we just need to get the emotion out of our body. By writing it down, we express it and witness it. We pay attention to ourselves and our feelings. For me, once the anger has been expressed, I feel relieved and happy and in balance again.

It's important to write stream of consciousness without stopping to think, self-edit, or be concerned with how the writing looks. Psychologists Ron and Mary Hulnick recommend NOT going back to re-read anything, but burning the pages when you are done.

I'll give you a sample from my journal (then I will burn it): "I am so angry and frustrated and lonely. I am so annoyed. I am so frustrated and angry and annoyed. I feel like I have no friends. No one emails me. No one calls me. I know this is another test and I am failing it. I feel like I have no power, no health. I can't get my fucking health back. I am so frustrated and annoyed. Why have I had cramps my whole life and no baby? It's so fucking unfair and annoying...."

You must keep writing until you feel a shift in your body. A change of the energy. Anger might be replaced by tears and then finally love and relief. It's important not to judge what comes out. If you judge it, then a part of you will try to repress it and then it will be stuck in your body!! Don't be ashamed! We all have a shadow side. That is part of being human. The shadow side must be expressed somehow. If you don't express it in writing, it might try to come out as an addiction or as a "nervous breakdown." These are just pent up emotions that need expressing. You can safely express them in writing. Otherwise, you might feel that you simply HAVE to answer that booty call or open the refrigerator. Trust me—writing it out is healthier!!

_____

_____

_____

The Joy Experiment

The Joy Experiment

blocks to joy

"Joy does not simply happen to us. We have to choose joy and keep choosing it every day."

– Henri Nouwen

I have been focusing on raising my levels of joy for six months now and I have to say, I am shocked at the results. First, it is possible to raise your joy levels. Measurably. Second, I realized I am the one who keeps blocking my joy. Over and over again!

I can't believe it! There I was, totally unhappy and miserable, blaming everyone in my life for the way things turned out, when—low and behold—I discover…it is *my* choice. I get to decide.

Yes, it's true. A lot is programmed into our DNA. The hair. The eyes. The sparkling wit. But there is also a lot that can be changed.

If depression is solely chemical, how did I stop being depressed? How did I stop wanting to die? Why do I now love my life?

It's because I did the work. I set the intention, I cleared the traumas, I reframed the beliefs, and now I am basking in the joy. Yes, it's a daily process. I do the breathwork every day. But now it's a joy to do it!

Now that I've cleared the big blocks. The big traumas. Like thinking I was unlovable. Thinking I was a waste of space. Thinking I wasn't wanted. Feeling like I couldn't endure the emotional anguish. Now that I've cleared all that garbage, now I see the smaller things I do on a daily basis that cut into my joy levels. I've listed the top joy blockers below…

JUDGMENTS

Judging myself and other people. I think Jesus said that was a "no no." But even if you don't believe in Jesus, it still feels bad. It always feels bad.

Here's what happens: I am driving along full of energy, excited about what a great show my chorus and I had in

Bakersfield. I'm in an a'cappella group and we compete every March in a regional competition. This was my first time. It is super fun. Everybody gets really dressed up—sequins and fake eyelashes. And then we sing our hearts out to a group of judges…just like American Idol. Except without Paula and Simon.

Anyway, I am driving home, riding high on the energy and camaraderie and all of a sudden I think, "I hope no one is mad at me that I didn't stay for dinner." Then I think, "Wow, those ladies put so much pressure on me to do group activities." Then I think, "It's not fair. I want to participate, but I can only do so much. I only have so much energy." Then I go even further, creating this huge NEGATIVE story in my head, "Boy, so-and-so is so judgmental. She's probably talking about me right now at dinner because I didn't stay." I created all this. Nothing happened. No one actually got mad at me or said, "You have to be at dinner." I wove this whole story in my head.
Why?

Because my body is still adjusting to being happy. It doesn't want me to go too far. The way you grow up sets your happiness level. Mine was set on low levels of joy and high levels of worry. These were the messages I got as a child: "Life sucks. Nothing is okay. Something bad is always going to happen. Someone is going to betray you. We are almost broke."

So, when things start going great in my life, I am compelled by my inner thermometer to find something wrong. So, I destroyed my great performance high by "judging" these women as "judging me."

Judging in any form feels bad in your body. If you judge yourself, if you judge others, it's basically just feeding the negative energy, or, the "pain body."

Originally, we needed judgments to protect ourselves. We divided people and things into right and wrong so we could pursue happiness and avoid pain. But this same mechanism that protected us in our youth can destroy us in our adulthood. Let me explain: the job of the ego is to keep us safe. Every time we are hurt or deprived, the ego rises up and creates a "rule" so we can avoid that pain in the future.

That is why we have "triggers." Our triggers are places where we've adopted rigid beliefs to avoid being hurt again. Some people's rules are: "I don't need anyone's help"; "Women want me for my money"; "Men aren't trustworthy"; and so on.

If someone accuses us of being "stupid," the ego creates a fervent desire to prove our intelligence. If you had a smothering mother, then your ego will react to women offering love as being needy and trying to control you. The ego isn't to blame. It is a powerful mechanism to keep us alive. However, it is so strong that it can imbed messages that ruin our lives by creating incredibly constricting rules.

The ego makes you judge people to defend or protect yourself.

But judging something as bad has a very powerful effect on your mind and body. Judging yourself or talking negatively to yourself can not only make you feel bad, but it can cause sickness, accidents, and—in the most extreme cases—even death.

This is because your body believes your thoughts and creates experience to match your beliefs.

JUDGEMENT WARNING
Judging carries a negative charge. It makes you feel bad. You can create boundaries and change your circumstances without labeling someone or something as bad or wrong. You can just imagine it isn't your preference. No energy. No label. No judgment.

We make judgments without even realizing we are doing it. Our thoughts stray and we categorize others, put ourselves down, and ruin our good mood in the span of two seconds. Judging others as "bad" or "wrong" only brings up negative feelings in the person judging. They might be irritating, but we feel the annoyance in our bodies. They are insensitive, but we feel the lack of respect. They are unfair, but we feel the anger.

Because I have been taking an hourly inventory of my moods, I have grown very aware of when my mood shifts. If I suddenly shift from positive to negative for no apparent reason, I ask myself what I was just thinking. Usually, there was some fleeting, supposedly inconsequential judgment I made just moments before, and that shifted my energy from good to bad. This is how we commonly live. Judging people in our society is as common as eating. We think we need to do it to protect ourselves. But really all we do is load up our body with mental and physical toxins. Is it really worth passing judgment on someone whose full life experiences you cannot possibly comprehend—just to feel bad in your body?? Sounds like a lose/lose proposition.

This doesn't mean you go along without distinguishing between what is good for you and what isn't. It is absolutely possible, and even essential, to say "yes" to some things and "no" to others, but we can do it without hanging a judgment on those things. I can still decide who I want to hang out with or what I want for dinner. I just don't put anyone or anything down to do it. I observe that a person has a certain kind of energy that makes me feel good, so I want that person as a friend. I observe that a certain person does not have the energy I want to be around (without making them "wrong" or "bad"), so I decide I won't spend a lot of time with that person. I don't need to label them as "narcissistic" or "self-righteous"—I can simply choose not to involve myself with them.

Recently, I went out with an adorable comedy writer. Each time we went out, we had an amazing time. But afterwards, he wouldn't call me. A week would pass until he would make contact again, and then we'd go out again and have another wonderful time. As much as I loved our dates and thought he had the perfect last name for me and my family, I observed that I want to be in a relationship with someone who calls me often. Without making him into the villain and me into the victim, I decided that this is not the relationship for me. And if he ever calls me again, I will let him know…

Judgments carry negative energy. Observations do not. So, how can you tell if you have a judgment about something? One way is to ask yourself if you are making someone or something else "wrong" or "bad." If so, it is a judgment. Another way is to feel your feelings. If the thought brings up negative feelings in your body (anger, guilt, fear, annoyance), then it is a judgment. If your body feels neutral or clear of negative energy, then it is an observation.

Luckily, there is an easy way to get rid of those judgments. It's called forgiveness.

Forgive yourself for judging the person or thing. This is a method I learned from spiritual masters Ron and Mary Hulnick while getting my Master's Degree at the University of Santa Monica.

If I become aware of judging someone or something, I immediately say, "I forgive myself for judging _____ as _____.
"I forgive myself for judging the women at chorus as judging me."
"I forgive myself for judging my ex as being an ass."

"I forgive myself for judging my mom as crazy."
At first, forgiving judgments can be overwhelming. We have so many. But each time you do it, you can actually feel the negative energy rise off of you.

Face it—you hurt no one but yourself when you think someone is "stuck up" or "too uptight" or "selfish." The thought only hurts YOU! It is in your mind and your body!

Experience the incredible relief of letting go of judgments! You can still protect yourself with observations. These have no charge on them. They don't fill your body with negative feelings.

I don't know about you, but I have frequently been in the situation where I judged someone and then a year later I found myself in their exact same position and found myself doing exactly what I judged them for doing. I had an old writing partner who I secretly looked down on for being supported by her father for ten years after college. She didn't work. I was working crazy hours and was jealous that she had time to workout, read, date men, and hang out with friends.

I also got a lot of pride out of the fact that I supported myself and was moving forward with my career. Well, years later, because I made some financial mistakes, I found myself in a predicament: I either needed to be supported by my father (with a loan) or sell my house. I choose to be supported by my father. I was so embarrassed. I had judged her for the exact thing I was now doing.

Don't worry: I forgave myself for all those judgments! And I learned my lesson. Now, if I am even tempted to judge someone, I think, "There but for the grace of God, go I."

If you really think about it, we are all doing the best we can with what we've been given. If someone beats their child, it is awful, but chances are they were beaten. If someone cuts you off in traffic, you don't know what pressure they are under, what priorities they've developed, what challenges they may have taking proper care of themselves and therefore others.

The best we can do is to not take things personally. I used to have a boss who was really mean. He would shout insults at people down the hallway. He would rip apart his writers' scripts in front of the production team calling veteran writers "hacks." I could only imagine how much criticism this man heard echoing in his own head. To be so mean and spiteful, I thought he really must have seriously angry, hateful demons telling him the same thing. He was projecting onto others what the voices were saying to him.

While he was firing me (and insulting me as he did it), I looked at him with compassion and thanked him for the opportunity to learn from him. He was shocked. He kept insulting me, and yes, I did cry when I got into the parking lot, but deep down, I knew it was his issue, not mine.

EXPECTATIONS

Every time I meet a moderately attractive man who isn't wearing a wedding ring, within five minutes I've imagined our wedding and carved out our entire life together—the fun vacations, the deep conversations, the romps in the bedroom, how long it will take him to propose (wow, three months…a world record), how many kids we'll have, what their names will be, what our disagreements might be about—and all before he finishes answering the question, "What do you do for a living?" Weird, I think, I can't believe I just had kids with a guy named Chuck. Then I learn what he does for a living. Weird, I think, I never imagined I'd be married to an IT guy named Chuck.

I wrote an entire movie about women's expectations of men and romance. It's called *Singleland* because that's where you'll live if you project all your fantasies onto someone else and expect him or her to live up to them.

We all have expectations—some are created by our parents, some are created by our culture, some are created by our advertising agencies, and others are created by well meaning friends. Some are even created by our own imagination, extrapolating on how great something might be.

Expectations block joy by blocking reality. If I am creating the perfect husband in my mind, I am not seeing and appreciating that thoughtful guy right in front of me. Instead, I am disappointed that he brought lilies instead of roses and I won't even notice the nice complement he gave me on my colorful skirt. (What? I like Roses! Lilies stain the tablecloth when they open.)

Expectations take us out of the moment. You can't appreciate what someone has to offer if you are not seeing them for who they are. This applies to every aspect of our lives.

If I expect my sister to call me back and I get upset with her for not responding within a week, then I completely miss the fact that she is going through a hard time when I do talk to her.

Because I expected myself to be rich and famous, win lots of awards (like Emmys and Oscars) and make the world a better place with my profound observations of life, I was unhappy writing on other people's TV shows. I wanted it to be *my* TV show. I didn't just enjoy my time. I didn't enjoy my colleagues because I was so obsessed with creating my own show. (It's really good—you should read it.)

The best thing to do with expectations is be aware of them and let them go. Sometimes it can help to recognize where they came from.

One way to let go of expectations is to be very present in your body. How do we do this? One way is to repeat the affirmation: "I am living in the present moment." If you drift off into a negative future fantasy or start worrying about the past, just bring yourself back with: "I am living in the present moment." You can anchor in this truth by taking inventory of what is actually going on in the present moment: I am typing; my arms are sore from working out; my tummy is ready to be fed; I am wearing a burgundy robe.

Another way to get present is through the breath.

Inhale deeply, allowing your stomach to expand and your diaphragm to lower so your lungs can fill to their full capacity and exhale, -- letting go of stress and expectations.
Inhale into your chest, opening and expanding your heart and exhale any tightness or protection.

Inhale into your chest and shoulders and release the weight of the world with the exhale.

Inhale into your head and let the swirls and gusts of air release the mind from working so hard.

Inhale into your legs, feet and toes and exhale anything that no longer serves you.

Inhale into your arms, hands and fingers and exhale all tension and stress.

Inhale into your stomach and release all fears.

Inhale into your entire body and exhale any leftover tension you no longer need.

The Joy Experiment

Bringing attention to each part of the body through the breath is a form of self-love and it feels amazing.

Anywhere you hold tension or tightness, bring the breath there and let it caress the space around the contraction.

Breathe into your neck, your genitals, your breasts, your intestines, and your lungs, exhaling anything that no longer serves you.

This breath feels delicious and brings you instantly into your body—and back into the present moment!
And that's where the joy is!

The next moderately attractive man I meet without a ring on his finger—I swear I will get his full name before I pick the kid's names. They can all be juniors.

RESISTANCE
Resistance is a HUGE BLOCK TO JOY. We all have resistance. Resistance occurs when you know you could do something that would be healthy for you, make you feel great, and probably increase your self-worth and value, but...

You are too tired,
You are too busy,
You are too angry,
You are too depressed,
You are too focused on your career,
You are too cool,

You don't believe you can change,
You're problem is chemical,
You're too fat,
You don't have the right thing to wear,
There's nothing wrong with you.

What is your favorite excuse?
I would heal my life, but

_____

_____.

I would do what is healthy for me but

_____

_____.

I would do the breathwork, but

_____

_____.

Resistance is another mechanism that the ego uses to keep
the mood thermometer in check.
What is really behind that resistance?
What makes you sit in front of the television instead of going
on a walk?
It is not laziness!
It is a lack of belief in yourself!
This is learned. This is not innate.
If you think you are not a valuable person, you are wrong!
If you think your life isn't important, you are wrong!
If you think what you do doesn't matter, you are wrong!
Your life is important.
You do matter.
Your life has value.

You have a purpose for being here.

Sometimes we just get off track. We get loaded down with negative thoughts and beliefs and we can't get off the couch long enough to disprove them. (You can do breathwork on the couch!)

I have a friend who has a terrible physical injury. She went to see a traditional Western doctor, but she won't even look into the possible underlying psychosomatic reason for her pain. She would rather be in pain than consider a new way of thinking.

This is her ego saying, "I would rather be right than have to alter my belief system. I would rather be right than examine my life. I would rather be right and in pain than admit I might need help or need to change."

Personally, my resistance takes the form of sleepiness. When a boyfriend wants to discuss an issue, suddenly I am soooo tired. It's only 6pm, but I'm exhausted.

Another form of resistance I've used in the past was "I have a migraine." No one can argue with me on the floor in the bathroom yacking up my dinner for hours. Though this is totally real—I am actually getting sick and dinner is making a reappearance—it is also a way to avoid doing something I don't want to do or seeing something I don't want to see.

If you are judging yourself for being overweight or for being an alcoholic or suffering from depression, forgive yourself.

Believe that you can change.
Believe that you can get off the drugs.
Believe that people will help you.
Believe that you don't need anti-depressants to feel good.
Believe in yourself!

As my good friend and teacher David Elliott always says, "You can out-create resistance."
"You feel the resistance and do the thing anyway."

The voice of the ego will try to talk you out of healing. It will tell you lies like, "You can't change. It is too hard. You don't have time. You have to hold it together for the kids. It will try to distract you with porn or financial crisis or your back going out.

OUT-CREATE THE VOICE.
TRY THE TECHNIQUES.
BELIEVE YOU CAN CHANGE.
BELIEVE YOU ARE WORTH CHANGING FOR.
IMAGINE YOURSELF COMPLETELY HAPPY.
OUT-CREATE THE RESISTANCE.

I'M TOO COOL

This is an epidemic in American society.

The need to fit in and be respected by one's peers has meant the death of many a drunk frat boy and the slow destruction of many a trapped housewife.

A lot of people won't even look at a self-help book or see a therapist because it's "not cool."

They would rather live miserable lives than be made fun of.

They would rather kill themselves with alcohol than walk into an AA meeting.

It's true—it takes courage to walk this path.

There's a lot of judgment in our society about terms like "healer" or "negative energy." New Age people are frequently the butt of Hollywood film jokes.

I was lucky because I was so miserable as a child that I didn't care about what anyone thought of me. This gave me a lot of latitude to do exactly what I wanted. I eventually began to care about other people's opinions of me, but by that time, I had grown comfortable being outside the mold (for the most part); so, even when I wanted to do something to impress someone else, I couldn't. I always have to do what is true for me.

"I'm too Cool" was never my issue. But I see it a lot. It's the handmaiden to resistance. My ten-year-old cousin won't dance at his cousin's wedding because it's not cool.

He can see all the fun he is missing out on, yet he'd rather be safe and not take a chance on making a mistake or being made fun of.

But here's what I don't understand:
The whole point of being cool is to impress people and the whole point of impressing people is to have friends and the whole point to having friends is… to be happy…so…
Why the rigmarole?
Why not just be happy and then have friends that accept you the way you are?
That way you are guaranteed for the happy plan to work. Otherwise, you're like a dancing monkey. No amount of tricks will satisfy your audience.

If you do anything for an ulterior motive, you can practically guarantee you won't get your desired outcome.
If you take a job because it is prestigious and you think it will impress the ladies, but you hate it…guess what? The job will not make you happy.

If you date a man because he looks good on paper, but you don't really feel anything… guess what? He will not make you happy.

If you focus on being happy regardless of who accepts it or approves of you, then you are guaranteed of the one thing that counts: Happiness.

You have to begin within.

Clear out the pain and then figure out for yourself what makes you happy.

It could be someone or something unexpected.

Like a'cappella singing for me. My cool friends make fun of me for being in a chorus, but I have so much fun that it doesn't matter.

Being cool will never make you happy.

Smoking and drinking to fit in will never make you happy.

Sleeping with the boss (for the wrong reasons) will never make you happy (for long).

Because anything you do to look good to others is not real. Ultimately, it doesn't feel right or good.

The only way to be happy is to ask yourself what makes you happy and do it. Although people may make fun at first, the moment they see how happy you are, they will want to do it too. Hmmm…the theme of High School Musical.

I've often thought about how to make it cool to meditate. Maybe an ad with Keanu Reeves sitting on a rock in Sedona, taking in the beauty, then the voice-over deeply intones, "When I meditate, my worries melt away and I am filled with joy. It's excellent."

Or, a commercial with Zac Efron doing breathwork. "After a long day on set, I take time to relax and rejuvenate with healing breathwork."

That would be cool if major movie stars did commercials for values like kindness and self-worth. I can imagine Brittany in a skimpy outfit saying, "Would it be so hard to love yourself today?" Or P. Diddy, in a suit, saying, "It's cool to love God. God loves you."

Maybe we are moving toward that. The Buddha has become an icon of peace in many households. And the Catholic cross reminds us of love and forgiveness.

I imagine a day where nobody smokes or drinks or over-eats, but instead gets high on breathing, blissing out on beauty, and laughing 'til they cry tears of joy.

WHO WILL I UPSET IF I AM HAPPY?
I remember being a teenager and heading out the door for an afternoon of cavorting with my gal pal, when suddenly my mother stopped me for some minor teenage infraction and grounded me. Knowing the punishment was unfounded, I said: "You don't want me to be happy, do you?" and she replied, "You're right. I'm not happy. Why should you be?"

For years, I was very careful not to be too happy in front of my mother. If I was in love, I wouldn't mention it because her next comment would be about how men can't be trusted or always leave. Being upset around my mother doesn't work either because she's used to winning at pity parties. If I said I was let go from a job, she'd tell me about someone who lost his child. If I said I broke up with a boyfriend, she'd tell me about an entire family accidentally wiped out in a gas explosion…while on vacation.

So, I used to stay very neutral around her. So neutral, in fact, that you might mistake me for a zombie. I replied in grunts, occasionally throwing in an "Oh really?" to spice things up. My mother's happiness meter is stuck lower than mine. So, it's natural that if things are going well, she would create issues in order to wipe out the joy and maintain the lower level of happiness.

Recently, I did a mega gestalt with a sinus infection that would not go away and discovered it was my body's way of punishing me for being happy. This was completely subconscious. I had no idea that the happier I became, the more the illness fought to suppress my happiness. Once I became aware of it, I reframed the limiting belief by using affirmations like: "It is safe to be happy"; "I am happy, healthy, whole, perfect, and complete"; and "I am free to enjoy perfect health and ecstatic happiness." Also, I set an intention every night to be healthier and happier tomorrow.

When I was younger, I told my mother she wasn't allowed to talk about negative things with me, and she retorted, "Fine, we can talk about superficial things if you want."
Happiness is not superficial. Peace is not superficial. Overcoming patterns that make a person ill is not superficial. Finding your life purpose and pursuing it is not superficial.

I have a friend who is spectacularly gorgeous, but used to have skin problems marring her beautiful face. When she looked deeply into the problem, she discovered that when she was younger her friends rejected her for being too good looking. She got so much attention that they didn't want her around. So, her mind created the acne to compromise her looks and allow her to fit in. As an adult, she no longer needed to play small and act to appease others. Once she processed the pain of the early rejections and let go of the false belief that she had to compromise her looks to make others happy, the acne cleared.

Not everyone in your life wants you to be happy. Not everyone wants you to be successful. But it's not healthy to compromise yourself in order to avoid upsetting someone else. Ultimately, it will make you sad and bitter anyway. Better to identify who allows you to be yourself and supports the highest vision of who you are—and focus on those relationships.

In healing, we often ask ourselves what is the benefit of this pattern of behavior? What do I gain by playing small or not shining? There is always a benefit to any behavior. If you know you are not living up to your potential, ask yourself why. How are you benefitting from playing it safe?

Then listen for the answer. Some common answers are, "I want to avoid heart break" or "I am saving you from rejection." But you also miss out on the lessons to be learned from trying and failing. And finally, you miss out on the eventual delicious joy of success. As an aside, my mom has gotten much better over the years, slowly releasing her limiting beliefs and allowing herself tiny happiness after tiny happiness.

I DON'T HAVE TIME
I don't have time to take care of myself.
I don't have time to eat right.
I don't have time for fun.
I don't have time to meditate.
I don't have time to spend on my relationships.
I don't have time to enjoy my life.

It is so easy to believe these lies, to believe there is not another minute in the day to take care of yourself or work on your issues.

But what does your body do when you ignore it? It gets sick and forces you to slow down. What do your feelings do if you don't listen to them and express them? They cause anxiety attacks. What does your mind do when you refuse to listen to it? It keeps you up all night shouting at you with insomnia. What does your spirit do when you repress your desires? It gets you fired from the job you hate, giving you plenty of time to pay attention to what you really want.

Pain is a corrective mechanism. If you are off of your path, you experience pain or numbness until you get back on track. You are on track when your body is filled with joy and your life delights you. The problem comes when people misinterpret pain. They draw conclusions about pain like "God hates me" or "all love comes with pain." When actually, the pain is loudly pointing at the misbelief you need to clear, or the aspect of yourself that you need to integrate—the part of you that is crying for love and attention.

It takes a leap of faith to move from survival consciousness to abundance consciousness. It takes courage to let go of the "shoulds" and "have to" and to focus on what would be truly nourishing and self-loving. Pain forces people to correct their path. You will either get sicker, get more addicted, need more anti-depressants, OR choose to heal yourself through taking corrective actions: letting go of misjudgments, forgiving yourself and others, starting on a path of self reflection, and doing what you love.

Sometimes people wait until they find out they are dying, or are so out of control that they can't go on.
I've never understood why people would rather suffer than meditate a half-hour a day and love life.
It's an easy equation.

<u>MEDITATE HALF-HOUR = BLISSFUL DAY</u>

Even ten minutes before you fall asleep can clear the day's slings and arrows. Let's look at the time benefits from clearing your blocks to joy:

- It saves you the time and energy of climbing the wrong ladder in your career.

- It saves you from the arguments caused by you projecting your pain onto someone else.
- It saves your body from having to break down to get your attention.
- It saves you time at work by connecting you to abundant creativity.

All the guidance and knowing we need is inside us; we just need to be able to hear it. And to do that, we need to clear away the negativity.

Instead of spending a night in the emergency room, take the time to do the breathwork every day and stay out of the emergency room altogether.

JOY WARNING!

If you don't respond to breathwork, there are literally hundreds of styles of meditation that can support you in clearing your mental, emotional, physical, and spiritual issues. If you don't respond to meditating, there are hundreds of other forms of energy healing that can release negative patterns and facilitate a happier life: Kundalini Yoga, Matrix Energetics, Ecstatic Dancing, Kunlun, Family Constellation, Tantra, and many, many more. Check out www.myalternativehealer.com to find a method that resonates with you.

BELIEVING THE BROKEN RECORD

When I was a teenager, I never thought my life would change. I thought everyone would hate me and I would be alone my entire life. I thought I was a waste of breath. I felt guilty when I created trash. I thought I would be miserable and want to die every day for the rest of my life, or that I'd actually kill myself.

I believed the broken record.
I believed that voice in my head that told me I was worthless.
And that voice is painful to listen to.
It was only when I turned twenty that I had this epiphany: I didn't have to live the way I was living. I could become anyone I wanted, with any belief system I wanted. I could change.

It was then that I decided to break the record.
I decided to change my perspective.
But I didn't have the tools I needed.
It took me twenty years to discover these tools.
I spent ten years in therapy, which was a very small Band-Aid on a very big wound.

Though therapy was a good first step, this wound was so much bigger than therapy had answers for.
I basically had to reconnect to my soul.
No small feat and nothing an hour of therapy a week could do.

I needed spirituality, which I finally found.
The point is this:
If you are not happy,
If you are not doing something to improve your life,
Then most likely, you are listening to the broken record.

Here are some other songs the record plays…
I can't change, so why bother?
My depression is chemical, so I need drugs to help me.
Life is hard and then you die.
I don't deserve to be happy.
I don't believe in energy work.
I don't even believe in God.
But you don't have to believe in God or anything for this to work. If you want to get better—if you want to be happy—that's all you need.

THE BROKEN RECORD SAYS:
I won't succeed, so why should I try?
That guy won't like me, so why should I try?
I can't get that job, so I'll complain about this one.
You get the idea.

SEE IT FOR WHAT IT IS.
IT'S CRAP and it's ruining your life.
Break the broken record!
It's probably not even yours!

MAKING IT WORSE
This occurs when we pile guilt or shame or anger on top of an issue. You frequently see this with addictive behavior. There's the acting out itself and then the pain that tries to correct the behavior and say "you are off course"… the hangover, the stomach ulcers, etc. And then there's the pain on top of the pain: the guilt of being an alcoholic, the self hatred of knowing you are destroying your body through

bulimia, the shame of cheating on a beloved partner from a sex addiction.

Doubling the pain makes it feel overwhelming.
The addict is already avoiding dealing with the original pain and now has twice the pain to process. This is why it is so difficult to recover from an addiction. It requires discipline and faith to refrain from the addiction and then courage and support to face the original issue.

FOCUSING ON OTHERS
Many people are great at recognizing someone else's issues. They have the perfect advice for how their husband could be a better person or how their neighbor should water their lawn (only Tuesdays and Thursdays!). Unfortunately, this is often a misguided effort to avoid taking responsibility for themselves and their own process.

I have a lot of compassion for advice-givers, as I am a recovered advice-giver myself. I wanted to fix everybody and save the world. I believe this stemmed from my past desire to save my mother from her depression. My spiritual teacher told me several times that my mother was on the perfect path for her. I couldn't understand how being miserable was a spiritual path, but my teacher said I didn't know what my mother's karma was or the purpose of her life.

What if all her misery was so that I could learn how to transmute energy from negative to positive? What if I was the reason she acted "crazy" because I needed to see through the lies of being abandoned and unloved. Well, that turned me around. And fast. If my mother had to be depressed so I could learn my spiritual lesson, then I needed to pick up the pace. I let go of needing to fix her and now see her as "perfect, whole, and complete." I don't worry about her. I protect my boundaries, but I don't label her behavior as "bad." It is what it is. And low and behold, her behavior has changed. Around me she focuses on being happy and embracing life, and for several months now we've had a lovely relationship.

Advice-givers were usually raised by unavailable or troubled parents; they trained for years in taking care of the needs of their mother and/or father. Subconsciously, they try to fix their parents in the false hope that once the parents are well, they can offer the child the love and support they craved for their whole lives. But nothing the child can do will change the parent. We cannot empower someone else. We can only show them the steps to empowerment and cheer them on as they take each step. People are responsible for themselves.

That is a universal law.

As Gandhi tells us, "Be the change you wish to see in the world." Any advice you are tempted to give someone else is usually the perfect advice for you. If you see a problem in the world around you, go inside and see how you can clear that issue in yourself. If you hate war or abortions, go inside and see if you have an internal war waging or where you have denied the joyful life of your inner child.

PROGRESS BACKLASH

"Before a dream is realized, the Soul of the World tests everything that was learned along the way. It does this not because it is evil, but so we can, in addition to realizing our dreams, master the lessons we've learned as we move toward that dream. It's at this point most people give up. It's the point at which, as we say in the language of the desert, one dies of thirst, just before the palm trees appear on the horizon."
- Paulo Coehlo

This is when you start to change and life seems better, and then something bad happens and you think, "I'm right where I started. I did all that work for no reason." You throw out the baby with the bathwater. You want to give up on healing because you backslid, you made a mistake, something went wrong, so why bother?

Often times, this is just the universe testing you to make sure you learned the lesson. It is important to keep going at this point. It is important to refrain from judgment; berating yourself for backsliding or not being where you want to be only creates more negativity and backward movement.

Freedom from that negative thought or habit could be just around the corner.

Another frustration I hear from my breathwork clients is, "I've worked on this issue so many times. I thought I was done with it." They recognized the issue, they took responsibility for it, they followed the pain back to the original wound, they grieved the pain, they identified the underlying misbelief and reframed it—and then the issue comes up again!

I hear you!!
I can't count the times I have dialogued with unworthiness. Many times for many years. And each time, I thought it was the last. The truth is that each time, I released a little more of the unworthiness and felt a little lighter than before. And now, I feel totally worthy and valuable, without a trace of the earlier feelings of unworthiness.

There were several layers that needed to be cleared: the body, the thoughts, the emotions, and the subconscious. The process is the same for all levels. Be patient. Be compassionate. Trust that you are moving forward. Feel the difference in your body from what you have cleared. Acknowledge your progress! Celebrate your victories!!

"How you are with the issue is the issue." – Ron and Mary Hulnick

DISTRUST OF AUTHORITY

Sometimes when we have been abused by authority, we rebel against it. I told my parents they were not my parents when I was 14. But the problem with this dynamic is that if you hate all authority figures, it makes it really hard to get help. The cause of the problem prevents the solution to it. Once a person has been abused by an authority figure, it is very difficult for them to get over it because any person striving to help is deemed an authority figure and thus, untrustworthy.

Losing that first relationship of dependability and trust creates an angry person who refuses all help (cuz they don't trust it will help) and so must "do everything on their own." Not only that, but their distrust extends from the person who first broke trust to their boss, to their teachers, and even to God.

"God didn't protect me from this person who hurt me so I can't trust God either." This is a conundrum. The expectation of being let down or hurt leads to that very reality. The chip on the shoulder from being hurt makes others defensive as well. So, the person with authority issues will inevitably work for the unfair boss, will get pulled over by the condescending police officer, and will spend hours on the phone trying to get a refund for $12.99.

This will be further proof of the injustice in the world and lackadaisical attitude of God. The people who feel most hurt will become skeptical of everything. They will see people as trying to get something from them. They will see kindness as manipulation and love as entrapment.

My friend grew up in Afghanistan during the Russian invasion. He is now very skeptical of all governments, thinking they are all corrupt. But he is also skeptical of anyone with any power. He distrusts authority of any kind, whether they are in politics or an energy worker or a psychologist. He can't allow anyone to know more than him because his unhealed trauma makes him believe that they could hurt him. So, he will listen to no one, respect no one, and only follow his own guidance. That would be okay if he weren't trapped by his own broken records.

Unable to receive feedback, he repeats his same issues over and over. But for him, to accept anyone else as an authority is the subconscious equivalent of putting his life in jeopardy. How can he change? He will have to learn to trust. He will have to trust someone to have greater insight than he does. This a real challenge for him. It also keeps him from being a leader. If he believes all authority figures are bad, he certainly won't allow himself to become one.

As I edit this, he too has changed and grown, getting a job where he witnessed firsthand how a government worked to help people and improve lives. Though he's still skeptical about authorities, learning to trust even one entity could help him expand his trust even wider. Maybe it will be enough to heal the underlying limiting belief that created his bad experiences with authority in the first place.

THE PERFECTIONIST
Many people suffer from this. They think they have to be perfect all the time to have any value. They can't stand the idea of crying out their feelings or looking at their issues. But this sets up a real problem because then the perfectionist only has two choices: never try anything new or deny, deny, deny. Never trying new things makes for a very stagnant life.

And being unable to admit to a mistake forces the perfectionist to cast blame onto others. They can never be at fault. It was someone else's mistake. If a person is blind to their mistakes, then they can't take responsibility for them, they can't forgive them, and they can't let go of them. Those denied mistakes get deeply buried in their bodies and turn into toxins. This is an exhausting and noxious cycle.

Mistakes are given a bad reputation. We should praise mistakes. We should prize falling down. We should appreciate someone for being vulnerable and taking responsibility. It is the only path to health. What perfectionists fail to remember is that their value is innate.

There is nothing they have to do to be valuable. Without having an intrinsic feeling of value, no accomplishment will be enough. There will always be something more you could have been or done. Value comes from being, not from doing. The antidote to being a perfectionist is to allow yourself to make a mistake, be with the feelings of discomfort that come up, and let them evaporate from your body into the nothingness from which they came.

I had a friend ask me how he could stop drinking so much. I quickly suggested Alcoholics Anonymous. He refused, insulted by the suggestion. He said, "I'm not an alcoholic, I just drink too much." In his peer group, it is considered weakness to go to a support group. Hopefully, his intention to drink less will have more power than his denial and he will have the courage to make a change. AA helps thousands of people break their debilitating pattern of addiction each year.

JOY WARNING—
To recognize if you have an addiction, stop doing that thing for 40 days. If you feel craving, obsessive desire, anger, or sorrow without it, then you are using that thing as a substitute for love. Maybe that was necessary when you were younger because you didn't have any other solutions, but now you are better off letting go of the substitute and discovering and experiencing real love.

BEING A VICTIM

This is a big one. How can you succeed if you identify yourself as a victim? How can you have the power to make changes if you view yourself as a victim? You can't. Yet so often we cling to our victimization like a favorite grandparent. I did this when I insisted that my ex-writing partner ripped me off $60,000 dollars. And the amount kept growing as I added in residual amounts and interest. I was so determined that she was the perpetrator and I was the victim. I was so betrayed! But holding that position only made me sick and angry in my body. She didn't care.

I spent years contemplating her betrayal and judging her as evil. But once again, the pain and anger were only in my body; they didn't affect her in the least. But now that I've cleared the pain and the judgments, I see how her supposed betrayal was the push I needed to get help. It was the extreme pain that I needed to make a change in my life. It impelled me into several healing programs. It inspired me to get my Master's Degree in Spiritual Psychology at USM. It necessitated learning to meditate. It opened me up to learning about energy and compassion. Through all these modalities, I learned to love myself, I healed my relationship with my mother and father, I reconnected to joy, and I rediscovered God. Easily worth $60,000.

But I had to take responsibility for my pain to get there. I had to let go of identifying myself as a victim and see how I contributed to the situation: by not speaking up, by denying the red flags, by not honoring my own value. Once I let go of my story, I learned so much about myself from what happened. Now, I can see how I set up the whole situation so that I could end that partnership, find my own voice, and write shows that I really believe in.

SUMMARY

These are the main joy blockers I have identified, but everyone is different. Are you aware of your blocks to joy? They are easy to locate. Think about a choice you just made or are about to make—one direction leads toward love and happiness, and the other leads toward something you "have to do" or "should do." Whatever justification you used to take the second road is your joy blocker.

It is amazing how many "needs," "shoulds," and "have tos" are just fear-based habits. Our parents, our society, or our early experiences of pain give us these limiting beliefs. Sometimes our dreams aren't even given a chance to be recognized because of our preconceived judgments about them. A common limiting belief is "I won't be able to support my family if I follow my dream." Maybe. But maybe you could support your family more abundantly. Maybe being happy is a better support for your family than being wealthy and angry all the time or killing yourself with a job you hate.

My psychology teacher recommends "three foot tosses," which are small action steps toward one's goals.
Do any of the above blocks to joy resonate for you?
You'll need to identify your blocks in order to clear them.
Here's a quick test:

It would make me so happy to _____

_____

_____

_____

_____

But I can't because_____

_____

_____

_____

_____

Now look at your reason why not and ask yourself what excuse you are using to block your joy? Is it valid? Where did this thought pattern come from? Did your mother/father tell you this as a child? Or is this a cultural message? Can you clear the underlying misbelief that created it? Are you brave enough to be more joyful? Use the space below to explore these questions and connect more fully to your joy!

_____

_____

_____

_____

_____

_____

_____

_____

_____

_____

_____

_____

_____

_____

The Joy Experiment

The Joy Experiment

learning to love myself

"I celebrate myself, and sing myself."

– Walt Whitman

When I was younger, I didn't know what self-love was. I couldn't feel it in my body. I could feel victory or pride or accomplishment, but not self-love. I didn't even know what it would feel like. I thought I understood what love was. I felt warmth and affection for my sister, my friends, and my pets growing up. I had strong, obsessive affection (and lust) for boyfriends over the years. I thought that was love because it was a strong positive feeling. But the moment I felt love for myself, I realized what I had missed out on for years. It was seeing myself with affection and compassion. It was appreciating everything that I am. It was seeing flaws and gifts and loving myself unconditionally. It felt like radiant, positive energy filling me up. It felt like 10,000 people applauding me. It felt like warm ocean waves caressing the inside of my body. It felt good!

Self-love Opportunity!
No time to love yourself? That's why God invented traffic. If you are stopped at a red light or in a line of traffic, take it as an opportunity to reflect on how fantastic you are.

Up until that point, I gave my love away (if I even knew what it was). At the age of six, when my sister was born, I saw how much everyone loved and adored her. I was among the worshippers. She was so cute and sweet. At that time, I jumped to a false conclusion: I thought she was more lovable than me.

From that moment, I established a pattern of other people's lives being better or more important than mine. That pattern haunted me throughout my life. It has caused me to be jealous of other women—a feeling that has caused me to ruin relationships. It has caused me to constantly look outside myself for love and approval. After all, if I value someone else above myself, then I will naturally need their approval so that I can feel good about myself.

It caused me to see other people's life paths as better than mine. My sister got married and had kids…so, her life must be better. She's more accepted by society.

I did the same thing with boyfriends. I always loved them more than I loved myself. I valued them higher than I valued myself.

In the past, I was thinking about how I much loved a certain man and how I couldn't be with him. And I suddenly thought: that is the way I should love myself—with the same level of passion and adoration. Why am I giving my heart to him? I need to cherish my heart. I need to love myself first. I need to choose myself first.

If I didn't value myself, how could anyone else?
But it's a challenge to make the transition. I spent years trying to feel the same way about myself that I felt about other people, like my sister. I loved her ardently. I loved her unconditionally. I saw her as a precious, miraculous angel. I felt like she could do no wrong. But this was a terrible misunderstanding of my own value.

I too was lovable.
I too was valuable.
I was worthy of friends.
I was worthy of affection.
I was worthy, period.

Yet I didn't feel that way. When we don't love ourselves we treat ourselves badly. We abuse our bodies by eating bad foods. We allow others to take advantage of us because we're desperate for love and attention.

This is the attention we must give ourselves. Self-love can be discovered within you if you try. I discovered my own self-love through a healer named Francesca Boring. The way she looked at me and regarded me in healing circles melted my heart. I felt her loving. My years of defenses (grown from not feeling lovable) dissolved. I felt loved. I felt valued. I felt like what I had to say mattered. I felt seen and heard.

This was a revelation. I then went to school for Spiritual Psychology and deepened in my practice of loving myself. There were so many layers of anger and sorrow to lift before I could feel the full vibration of self-love. (For others, this might be layers of self-blame or shame or self-loathing). I used the Pranayama breathwork to clear these misunderstandings about myself.

I am perfect just the way I am. I am a glorious child of God. That is true and it is also true that it feels better to love myself than not to. It feels better to value my gifts than to bury them or mock them. It feels better to treat myself like a Goddess than to treat myself like trash. It feels better! I am more productive. I am more creative. I get paid more (though I know my value is innate and has nothing to do with what I get paid). The world reflects my positive beliefs back to me. I'm not talking about being egotistical or self-centered. I am talking about valuing yourself.

That is the healthiest thing anyone can do for themselves, their family, their community. When we truly love ourselves, we have love to give to others. When we truly love ourselves, we are in acceptance of everything.

When you love yourself, you don't get upset when people misunderstand you or reject you or fire you, because you know your true value. It comes from within. It is unshakable and no one has power over you. They can't manipulate you by giving or withholding their love. They can't control you by valuing you and then taking that value away. You are solid. You come from a place of love. You remain in the loving with yourself no matter how the outer world reacts to you.

Usually, when you are loving yourself, the outer world will reflect that self loving back to you—people will be attracted to you, companies will value your contributions, and everyone you meet will smile and talk to you like an old friend. If this isn't the case, the universe might be testing you. Stay in self-loving and you will pass the test every time! So how can you fall in love with yourself?

That's really the purpose of this book.
Clear the misunderstandings.
Forgive the judgments.
Lift the negative energy.
And feel the love that is natural underneath it all.

Here are a few other practices to support you in connecting with your self-love:

    1.   Find a picture of yourself as a baby. Take time every day to look at yourself with loving, giving

yourself unconditional love. (This is a process. It may take time to build up to looking at yourself lovingly. You can start with a few seconds and build to several minutes.)

2.   Make a list of all the things you don't like about yourself (that you judge yourself for) and say "Even though I _____ (feel fat, act mean, judge other people), I still unconditionally love and approve of myself. (You can say it, even if you don't mean it. The words themselves will start to shift your energy and thoughts.) Example, "Even though I act immature, I still unconditionally love and approve of myself."

3.   Gestures of Self Love. Act "as if" you love yourself. The mind doesn't know the difference, so the body accepts these acts as self-loving. Take yourself on a date, give yourself attention, buy yourself a present, exercise, get a message, etc. Do things for yourself that make you feel good. Treat yourself as precious, and you will begin to feel the truth of your preciousness.

4.   Try my self-love breathwork meditation. It is specifically designed to help you release negative feelings toward yourself and align with positive ones. www.joyinfinite.com/

5.   Create an affirmation for how you want to feel about yourself. An affirmation works like an intention—the universe shifts to make it true. Post the affirmation everywhere you will see it, say it first thing in the morning, before you fade off to sleep, and

several times throughout the day. Here is an example: "I am falling in love with myself, seeing my deep inner and outer beauty, and appreciating all the gifts I bring to the world every day."

6.   Transfer your love. If you have trouble giving love to yourself, here is an easy way to learn how to do it. First, think of someone you love (or a pet that you love). For me, I use my little dog Dickins. I can instantly feel so much love for him. Then I picture myself at the age that needs love. Me last night. Me at age 14. In this circumstance, it was me at the age of six. I hold the feeling of love I have for Dickins and I apply it to me as a child. I can see that little girl filling up with the love I am sending. I can feel how her feeling loved affects me now.

Try one of these exercises now:

_____

_____

_____

_____

_____

_____

_____

The Joy Experiment

_____

_____

_____

_____

_____

_____

_____

_____

_____

_____

_____

_____

_____

_____

_____

_____

_____

loving the shadow

**"The most terrifying thing
is to accept oneself completely."**

– Carl Jung

Just when I thought I loved myself, I had a shocking
revelation.
I was only loving half of myself.
I was loving the good stuff, the sweet part, the smart part,
and the productive part.
At the same time, I was hating the sad part, the angry
screaming part, and the relaxed, fun part.
I figured this out through a number of projections and my trip
to Maui.

On my trip to Maui, my mind wouldn't stop yelling at me.
"You can't afford this."
"How can you enjoy this so much when there is work to be
done."
"I think you might be lazy."

I had to struggle to let go of these broken records and allow myself a week's vacation to do nothing but enjoy.

I forced myself at every moment to do nothing but enjoy. Workaholism runs in my family and I had it for a few miserable decades, so the message I received was that if you relax EVER, you are lazy.

But that is ridiculous. It is healthy to relax and do nothing. It is essential to life to enjoy it.

But my point is that I was still holding judgments about the negative side of myself.

I was still embarrassed if I cried or was jealous.

I had a lot of time to practice accepting being sick, as I was sick for three weeks in April.

When I gave those parts of me a voice, they all said they felt like I shunned them and tried to bury them. Anger felt like it never got to be heard. Sadness wanted to be loved. Sickness felt that I looked down on it. Relaxation wasn't even speaking to me prior to my Maui trip. My shadow needed attention.

I had been trying to cut out parts of myself instead of listening to them. No wonder sickness was holding a rein of terror and anger was flaring out at the expedia.com phone operators and my eyes were literally tearing all the time for no reason.

So, I had to deepen my love. I had to hold anger lovingly and listen to it. Anger almost always turns into sadness when you pay gentle and loving attention to it. (I mean, after it tells you to f*ck off a few times.) Then holding sadness, I found my inner child, Melanie, (I refer to her as Melanie because that was my name at the time) at age 6, tucking my mother into bed in a chair she was sleeping in because she had pneumonia. That little girl was scared of losing her mother. She felt like no one was there for her. So, in my meditation, I held her for a long time.

I imagined myself at that age. In my mind's eye, I took Melanie into my arms and showered her with love and attention.

When you love these shadow elements, an amazing thing happens. They change. Resistance becomes assistance. The Protector that kept people away can change into the enforcer who helps you complete projects.

These elements are created in us for a purpose and once that purpose is served and the element believes we are safe, that energy can be used for anything.

The key is to acknowledge it and not deny it. In the past, I never wanted to admit that I could get very angry or that I cried a lot. But now I treasure these aspects of myself (though the more loving attention I give them, the smaller they get). I see how necessary they are in the process of life. Reacting with shame or denial to any impulse will only solidify that impulse and make it stronger. When I denied my anger, it would build up for months until suddenly I would explode on someone dear to me, literally screaming at the top of my lungs. Usually it ended the relationship, and often, the person had no idea there was an issue because I had buried my feelings under a false calm and happy demeanor.

Sometimes it is hard to talk to these aspects.
Sometimes they have been so punished and shamed that they cannot even speak.

They hide behind the craving to drink or behind psoriasis (or some other physical ailment).

They wouldn't dare express themselves because they know they will get hit or sent to their rooms alone or mocked.
Some people have a very unhealthy belief that being sad or angry is bad. This condemns their feelings and doesn't allow the person to experience their true, real feelings. Imagine a lion denying his roar, thinking it "wrong" or "bad." Humans were born with emotions to guide them. If we aren't in touch with how we really feel, we can go far off course.

SHADOW WARNING–
It is important to note when you're experiencing your own energy and when you're experiencing someone else's. A good test is to take responsibility for the feeling in question. You can do this by saying, "I take responsibility for the depression (or whatever it is) in my body." If it is yours and you take responsibility for it, you will feel an immediate emotional connection to it. Sometimes it will even release as soon as you own it.
However, if this is someone else's energy that you have picked up, it will be challenging for you to process. I recommend the energy

ritual on p. 64 to release someone else's energy and take back your own.

Luckily for me, the breathwork helps to open me up to my feelings. I have always been in touch with crying, but I got in touch with the other aspects as well. I was in touch with sickness everyday for three weeks because it literally would not go away and I wasn't going to suppress it again with antibiotics.

I feel like I've reintegrated my shadow side one self-counseling at a time. When I become aware of a feeling that in the past I would have suppressed, I make time for it. I set aside some time in the day to speak with it. If you are experiencing anxiety, it is probably covering up a deeper emotion, like anger, fear, or sorrow. Anxiety marks the tension within us to feel the feeling and at the same time suppress it.

So, I set aside time, and then I give it a voice.
I was speaking with "fear of failure" the other day and I found that it wasn't really "fear of failure," it was actually just my little girl who wanted some attention. I gave her attention and "fear of failure" disappeared.

SHADOW WARNING #2
If the energy you are releasing feels too dark and overwhelming, I recommend going to a certified breathwork facilitator or a trusted energy worker to support you in releasing it.

The Joy Experiment

As we have all experienced, emotions and shadow elements are multi-layerd. This is a process of peeling the onion. You may have to talk to anger a hundred times before it feels it has enough attention to relax. We are dealing with emotions that have been buried for decades. It was too scary to express them as children, but to be fully alive and in love with ourselves, we need to give them attention now.

EXERCISE: Bring up a quality that you dislike about yourself. Maybe you judge yourself as lazy or anal or an asshole. Give that aspect a voice. What does it have to say to you? Really let it speak. Don't censor yourself. Allow that aspect to express its feelings. Ask the aspect questions like: When were you created? What happened at that time? What purpose do you serve? Chances are, deep inside that aspect, there is a hurt child wanting to be loved. After you listen to the aspect and understand where it is coming from, see if you can offer it some love. Try it now...

The aspect I dislike about myself is

_____

_____

_____

_____

_____

_____

The Joy Experiment

The Joy Experiment

CHAPTER NINE:

forgiveness

"Forgiveness is a gift you give yourself."
– Suzanne Somers

I had a lot of shame. I had a lot of blame. I was always asking "Why?" Why did I have such a hard life? Why was I struggling? Why was my mother always depressed? Why did she put it on me? Why did I have no friends? Why wasn't I married?

As we know, from chapter 7, these were all judgments. Negative judgments I put on myself, my mother, my father, and my ex-boyfriends. (I put a lot of judgments on them.) Sorry, boyfriends!

While I was writing this, I had a lot of shame because my father was supporting me. Because of a large financial mistake I made, I had to sell my house at a huge financial loss or borrow money from my dad to pay the mortgage. I borrowed the money.

So, what good will a feeling of shame do me?
Is it going to help me finish the feature film I am writing?
Well, I can use a little bit of the shame in the lead character as she becomes empowered. But in general, there is nothing shame is going to do besides depress me. If I am depressed, then I can't write, and if I can't write, I don't have new spec scripts for my agents to market me or to sell. If I don't have new specs, it's harder to get a new writing job. You see where I am going. If I beat myself up for this, it doesn't help me use the time creatively. If I continue feeling badly, then I can't even use the time to socialize and have fun.

So what do I do?
I identify the judgment: I am judging myself as bad for being supported by my dad at this age.

Then I forgive the judgment: I let go of it. I cancel it to the universe.

I forgive myself for judging myself for being supported by my dad.

And there are lots of underlying misinterpretations that go along with this.

I forgive myself for judging myself as not a good enough writer to get another writing job.

I forgive myself for judging myself for buying a house with my boyfriend.

I forgive myself for judging myself as not financially responsible.

And just like that—the pain is gone. The weight from this judgment is lifted. The jail I created for myself is opened up and I am set free.

You can set yourself free.
It is so easy.

I do the world a disservice if I continue to wallow in shame and pain.

The truth is, I am not trusting the universe if I am judging where I am or what I am doing.

I can learn from my mistakes without judging myself as bad. The truth is, the universe is supporting me (both through my dad and then through a new job).

It knows exactly what I need to do each day, exactly what my experience needs to be.

The universe is working for the highest good at all times. I have faith that I am meant to use the time to write this book.

And when it is time to get paid again, I will get paid. I am so grateful for the universe's support through my father. Having just cleared this judgment, I am looking out my back window at the rolling green hills of Mt. Washington, the white clouds interspersed with blue sky, and the tranquil palm trees rustling in the wind.

That is, I am full of joy. I feel a tingling on my shoulders, my heart is full of love, and I feel aligned with the world. I feel like I am on the perfect path for me.

So, what judgments are weighing you down?
Are you ready to be free?
Are you ready to release judgments so you can live in joy and relish the moment?
We don't know why things happen. We don't know why people act a certain way.
But if we put negative interpretations on things and people, we fill ourselves up with negativity.
The moment I make a judgment about myself or someone else, that judgment raises bad feelings in MY body.
Why would I want that?

The moment I forgive myself for the judgment, I feel that negativity lift and leave my body.

Try it.
Forgive something.
Forgive yourself for judging meditation as weird.
I forgive myself for judging meditation as weird.
Can you feel the weight lift?
Can you feel the tingle of joy replacing that space?
Don't worry that you won't be able to make decisions without judgments. You can make even better decisions because they won't be heavy with negative energy.

So, recently, I was on a date with an adorable fella—I mean, hot. And at the end of the date (we were on a retreat in Ojai), he brought several open bottles of wine back to his tent.
Now, I could have judged him as an alcoholic, but I didn't.
What I did was observe his behavior.
I didn't make it wrong or bad.
As much as I wished he were a tea toteller like myself.
I merely observed, and then concluded that I probably wouldn't mesh well with someone who drinks this much.
No blame.
No judgment.
No arguing with reality.
He is this way and I am a different way.
A decision is made without the weight of judgment.
The rest of the story is that when I told him why I didn't want to date him, he told me the bottles were for his wine-tasting friends. Oops!

So, I forgive myself for making an uninformed decision.
Live and learn.

Get the idea?
So, what is trapping you?
What do you need to let go of?
Mean boss?
Thankless job?
Unhappy childhood?
Start thy self-forgiveness.

Anyone can practice it. From any religion. All it means is that you're letting go of blame.
The fear around forgiveness is loss of protection.

"If I forgive my ex-writing partner, then she will rip me off again."

But I've learned that I protect myself even better without fear and judgment.

I protect myself by making self-nurturing decisions.
This doesn't require someone to be bad or wrong.
All it requires is for me to evaluate what is good for me.
Pretty easy to do when you are aligned with spirit and accepting messages from your Higher Self.

Forgiveness doesn't mean no one is responsible for their actions. Quite the opposite—it means I am taking responsibility for clearing this pain or negativity I house in my body.

If you did something you consider bad, forgiving yourself is the first step to making reparations to others.

In my most recent break-up, I was a bit of a bitch. Now, I had good reasons for my anger and my approach, but ultimately, it just caused the pain to go on longer and get really messy. Once I forgave myself for the mistakes I made, I was able to apologize for being such a bitch. It doesn't mean that I was at fault or that I was the only one who behaved badly in the situation. I just took responsibility for my part. Once I cleared the self-blame and disappointment around the way I acted, I had more self-esteem to take responsibility for my actions and make reparations.

FORGIVENESS OPPORTUNITY!
FORGIVENESS WORKS EVEN IF YOU DON'T BELIEVE IN IT. JUST TRY SAYING THE FORGIVENESS OUT LOUD OR IN YOUR HEAD AND FEEL THE SHIFT IN YOUR ENERGY.

If you need help identifying where you need to forgive, ask yourself, What am I afraid of? Or, Who am I mad at? Negative emotions in your body will guide you to what needs healing.

You can forgive anything.
It doesn't mean you condone it or will allow it again.

It only means you rid yourself of the negativity associated with what happened.

You are free and clear.

If you want support in forgiving someone or something, try my Forgiveness meditation found on the Joy Infinite website.

I forgive myself for judging myself as _____

_____.

I forgive myself for judging myself as _____

_____.

I forgive myself for judging myself as _____

_____.

I forgive myself for judging myself as _____

_____.

I forgive myself for judging myself as _____

_____.

I forgive myself for judging myself as _____

_____.

I forgive myself for judging myself as _____

_____.

I forgive myself for judging myself as _____

_____.

I forgive myself for judging myself as _____

_____.

I forgive myself for judging myself as _____

_____.

I forgive myself for judging _____

as _____.

I forgive myself for judging _____

as _____.

I forgive myself for judging _____

as _____.

I forgive myself for judging _____

as _____.

I forgive myself for judging _____

as _____.

I forgive myself for judging _____

as _____.

I forgive myself for judging _____

as _____.

I forgive myself for judging _____

as _____.

I forgive myself for judging _____

as _____.

I forgive myself for judging _____

as _____.

I forgive myself for judging _____

as _____.

I forgive myself for judging _____

as _____.

CHAPTER TEN:

connecting to your higher self

"Joy is an attitude; it is the presence of love - for self and others. It comes from a feeling of inner peace, the ability to give and receive, and appreciation of the self and others. It is a state of gratitude and compassion, a feeling of connection to your higher self."

– Sanaya Roman

Growing up, I had a lot of voices in my head. They argued constantly. What to do? What to wear? They were critical and abusive, calling me names and making me feel like I was never enough. These were the messages I picked up from example and learned from others. These voices were debilitating and caused a lot of unnecessary crying and upset. They said things like "You're so fat"; "You're so stupid"; "You're such a failure." (No baby thinks of him or herself as a failure.) It almost makes me laugh now seeing how mean I was to myself.

When my Women's Studies teacher told me I was smart in 12th grade, I clung to that like a lifeline. One person believed in me. It was all I needed to believe in myself. I became a triple major: Philosophy, English, and Theater, I proved to my family, the world, and to myself that I was not stupid or a failure. This, however, was ego driven. My ego needed to feel better. It needed some certificates to show people. Even though exterior compliments and feedback can save us in times of trouble, it is better to find your own self-value inside yourself.

Deep, deep, deep inside, buried under years of programming, you have a wise, magnificent self that can give you all the love, attention, and guidance you need. That Higher Self sees your true value, knows your life purpose, and can guide you to take the correct action on your path. That compassionate self can act as the unconditionally loving father and mother you always wanted.

That self can actually re-parent you by giving love to all your wounded places. That self is in touch with higher energy forms, whether you call them love, the universe, nature, energy, spirit, Allah, God, or angels. That part of you ripples with the same vibration that created the cosmos. In moments of bliss, great joy, and unlimited happiness you have touched that part of yourself.

My ability to get in touch with my inner wise one took years.

Now I have her with me constantly if I need love or support. My Higher Self holds me when I feel sick or sad. She stands by me when I make mistakes. She loves me unconditionally, even if I fart or vomit or do something embarrassing or lay in bed for a day. She is always there telling me "It is okay" and "You will get through it."

She also guides me on what scripts to write and what websites to create. She pours information from the collective unconscious into me so I can create funny, powerful TV shows with it. She guides me to see the higher purpose in any obstacles that show up in my life. (Though I don't really see them as obstacles anymore—just life lessons.) She smiles at me in the mirror and tells me I am beautiful. She guides me to act lovingly to myself and others.

As I said, it took a number of years to fully develop this aspect of myself. I had a lot of help. I went to school for Spiritual Psychology at the University of Santa Monica where we trained as a counselor as well as cleared issues as a client. As the counselor, I practiced being with touch with my inner guide, and I practiced being in a state of loving grace through which wisdom could flow.

I also developed this aspect of myself with healer David Elliott in his breathwork teacher-training program. And actually, this aspect grew and strengthened with every workshop and healing modality I did. I was lucky to have magnificent, loving teachers to see what the Higher Self looks like. Eileen Kenny, Francesca Mason Boring, Ron and Mary Hulnick, Hazel Williams-Carter, Charu Morgan, Dawn Cartwright, and many, many more contributed to my growth.

HIGHER-SELF WARNING!
*Remember that your Higher Self is **always** loving, accepting, and compassionate. If you hear any negative messages, realize this is not your Higher Self, but a part of you that wants to be heard. Don't allow your Higher Self to be confused with your Inner Critic or Inner Disciplinarian.*

This isn't to say you can't uncover this aspect by yourself on a tropical island. You can!

This part of yourself develops naturally as you learn to love yourself. The aspect with which you are applying love to yourself is your Higher Self.

The importance of getting in touch with your Higher Self is that he/she can help you reintegrate all the other aspects. As mentioned before, each time we were wounded as children, the ego created a defense mechanism to avoid that pain in the future.

Those defense mechanisms control us. They are our addictions. They are our "rules." They are aspects of us that are inflexible. They are our wounded inner child masquerading as an asshole, a bitch, an angry driver, a shopping addict, an impatient customer, etc. Our inner wise one can give the defensive ego the massive love it needs to heal the issue so the trigger can disappear. Our inner wise one can love our inner wounded child until the misbelief about ourselves is cleared and all that is left is truth.

The truth of who we are: Amazing. Divine. Beautiful. Miraculous. Good. Loving. Love.

EXERCISE: Meet Your Higher-Self Meditation.
I invite you to record this meditation and listen to it in a quiet, private place.

The meditation is adapted from Piero Ferrucci's "Inner Dialogue" meditation from his book *What We May Be*.

MEDITATION: Lie down on a bed or yoga mat with nothing under your head. You can use an eye pillow or blanket to be comfortable. Close your eyes.

Now imagine riding a waterslide from your head down into your heart. Picture yourself in your brain jumping onto the slide and riding it past your eyes—whoosh—past your ears, down your throat, swirling and twisting in the flow of water, then down past your shoulders until you plunge into the expansive pool in your heart.

Set an intention to meet your Higher Self and feel the compassion and love of your Higher Self.

Picture yourself on a summer morning in a field. The sky is bright blue and there are flowers all around you. Feel your feet on the ground. Experience the wind caressing your cheeks. You feel a sense of readiness and expectancy. You see a mountain ahead of you. Looking at its summit gives you a sense of extraordinary elevation.

You decide to climb the mountain. You begin by entering a forest. You inhale the delicious smell of pine trees and sense the cool, dark atmosphere. As you leave the forest, you enter a steep path. Walking uphill, you feel the muscles of your legs working. Your heart beats and you can feel your blood circulating throughout your body.

There is a steep incline on the path. You use your hands to climb and grab branches of a tree to pull yourself up. Now you see that you are getting close to the top of the mountain. You feel a sense of elevation; the air is fresher and the surroundings are still. You keep climbing...finding yourself in a cloud. Everything is white and you can only see the mist that envelops you. You feel the particles of mist on your face. You proceed very slowly and carefully, barely able to see your feet.

Soon the cloud dissolves, and you can see the sky again. Up here, everything is much brighter. The atmosphere is extraordinarily clean, the colors of the rock and sky are vivid, and the sun is shining warmly. You are ready to move on. Climbing is easier now; you seem to weigh less and you feel attracted to the top and eager to reach it.

As you approach the top of the mountain, you become filled with an increased sense of height. You pause and look around. You can see other peaks surrounding you, the forest below, and a field in the distance.

You are now on top of the mountain, on a vast plateau. The silence here is complete. The sky is a very deep blue. Far off, you see someone coming toward you. He or she appears as a small luminous point in the distance. As the radiant being moves toward you, you can feel this being is wise and loving, ready to listen to what you have to say and tell you what you want to know.

The presence of this being gives you strength and joy. You see the wise being's face and beautiful smile and feel an emanation of loving kindness. You feel your body relax and let go of tension. You look into the wise being's eyes and recognize your own. You see this is a radiant version of yourself: your essence—your perfect, ideal self.

Your Higher Self comes toward you and greets you, wrapping his or her arms around you. Your Higher Self has something to tell you. Listen to what they want you to know. (Allow 1 minute of silence.)

Thank your Higher Self for the message. If you have a question for your Higher Self or need guidance about something, go ahead and ask for it now. Listen as your Higher Self responds. (Leave 2 minutes of silence on the recording for the answer.)

Your Higher Self has a gift for you. He or she pulls out a gorgeous, intricately decorated box. Your Higher Self tells you that inside the box is a symbol for you to know that she or he is always with you and loves you unconditionally. Open the box and see what the symbol is. (Leave 20 seconds of silence on the recording.) Thank your Higher Self for reminding you that he or she is always with you.

Now imagine yourself merging with your Higher Self. Step into his or her radiant energy. Feel what it feels like to be your Higher Self. Feel all the compassion, love, and joy of your Higher Self. Let the energy wash through every cell and every organ. Feel yourself radiating with the beauty of your Higher Self.

When you are ready, feeling your higher self in your heart, and find the path down the mountain. Your Higher Self is going to go with you wherever you go. Start down the mountain, and enjoy the sunlight on your face as you walk. Enjoy the feeling of your feet connecting to the earth. Feel the warmth of the wind caressing your body. Feel a smile spread across your face. The path down is much easier and you reach the bottom quickly.

As you walk back through the forest, you feel yourself beautiful, content, and aligned. The scent of jasmine and roses waft over you as the forest opens up to the field—now in full bloom. You lie down in the field to rest and integrate all that you learned and experienced.

As you enjoy the smells and comfort of the field, acknowledge yourself for giving this gift of time and loving to yourself.

Now that you are connected to your Higher Self, you can always ask for guidance. Your Higher Self can protect you when you process negative energy and support you when you let go of patterns that you no longer need. Your Higher Self is always available to guide you in your mind or in writing. I've included a counseling session with my Higher Self so you can experience the nurturing and support that my Higher Self gave me.

SELF-COUNSELING: I had a sinus infection for 6 weeks. Besides the runny nose and phlegm, it created an enormous pressure in my head and ears. In this self-counseling, a part of me is very upset about being sick; my Higher Self guides that aspect to express itself in order to get to the underlying feelings and misunderstandings. The aspect is just that: a part of me that was hurting and needed attention. These emotions were deeply buried in my subconscious, and they needed to be released so that the whole of me could feel loving and joyful.

SICK ASPECT (SA): Help me. It hurts. I can't take it anymore. Release me from this pressure. I can't stand it. It is relentless.

HIGHER-SELF (HS): Hi Sweetheart. What is the pressure?

SA: Pressure to perform. To keep going. To dance like a monkey.

HS: Who is putting this pressure on you?

SA: You are. Constant pressure. I'm going crazy. I can't take it. My head is about to explode.

HS: What do you want me to do?

SA: Leave me alone. Go away. Stop pressuring me.

HS: Can you tell me more about the pressure?

SA: Help everyone. Save everyone. Do everything noble and right. Don't drink. Don't smoke. Don't eat gluten. Don't eat dairy. Don't sleep around. Behave. Behave. Behave.

HS: What do you want to do? Those things make you sick…

SA: I make you sick regardless of those things so… God help me. God help us. I can't take it anymore. I want out. I'm sick of being sick. I refuse to be sick anymore. Not one second more. Just stop it.

HS: I'm sure it's frustrating.

SA: Help me, help me get out of it. Help me stop it.

HS: What do you want me to do?

SA: Kill me. Put me out of my misery.

HS: I am not going to kill you. That would kill the whole of us.

SA: Kill me.

HS: Why do you want to die?

SA: It's a miserable life. Even if you get happy everyone else wants to tear you down. I'm sick of it. I welcome death.

HS: Sweetheart, you have a limiting belief about life that you need to let go of.

SA: It's true. Life is miserable. I hate people. I want out.

HS: What are you feeling?

SA: Sad. Neglected. Hopeless. Useless. Miserable.

HS: Dear One, what happened to make you feel this way?

SA: Life happened.

HS: When do you first remember feeling this way?

SA: Age 5. Tucking mom into bed with pneumonia. No one was there for me. I had to put myself to bed.

HS: I can see how that would be hard.

SA: It was. I thought mom was going to die and I loved her so much.

HS: Yes, you were just little and you needed to be loved.

SA: No one loved me because the only person who did was sick.

HS: I'm sorry that happened.

SA: No one cared for me.

HS: I know, Melanie, let it out.

(The sick aspect changes into me at age 5. As I mentioned before, my name then was Melanie.)

M: I want my mommy!

HS: Yes! What else?

M: I hate my mommy for not being there.

HS: I hear you. What else?

M: I'm so lonely. I have no one. I am sad and there is no one to comfort me.

HS: You have me now.

M: I want my Mommy.

HS: Yes, I hear you. Let it out.

M: Why is there no one to love me?

HS: Dad was scared of Mom and Mom was sick and couldn't think straight.

M: I'm scared I am all alone.

HS: I am here with you Sweetheart; you are not alone.

M: I wanna cry.

HS: Go ahead and cry.

M: I'm so angry and frustrated and confused. What is going on?

HS: I'm here for you little one. Let me hold you.

M: Why would you want to hold me? I'm unlovable. Nobody loves me.

HS: That's not true. I love you very much. You are very lovable to me.

M: I am?

HS: Yes, you are.

M: Then why does no one love me. Why are my brothers mean and my dad non-existent?

HS: It has nothing to do with you Sweetheart. They are going through their own experiences.

M: But I want love and attention.

HS: I know and I am here to give it to you. Just you. I love you. You are an adorable little girl. So precious.

M: Where were you before?

HS: I wasn't developed enough to comfort you. But I'm here now.

(In my imagination, Melanie cries in my arms. My body relaxes.)

M: That feels so good.

HS: Yes it does. I love you little one.

M: Life could be okay.

HS: Yes.

M: I am not alone.

HS: Nope. I am here for you.

M: I feel happy.

HS: That's good. You should feel happy. You're young and you have your whole life ahead of you.

M: Don't ever leave me again. I don't want to be alone again.

HS: I won't. I am here for you whenever you want me.

M: I don't want to be sick anymore.

HS: Let's time travel back to when you were 5. I clear all vows, promises, oaths, contracts, and agreements to be sick, I clear all ideas of wanting to die and send them to the dark side of the moon to be dissolved back into the nothingness from which they came. I pull out all the hooks and bury them in the earth. I flood your body with light so that all the wounds are healed.

M: Much better. I love you.

HS: I love you too.

Make notes about meeting your Higher Self:

_____

_____

_____

_____

_____

_____

_____

_____

_____

_____

_____

The Joy Experiment

CHAPTER ELEVEN:

the challenge of change

"Healing takes time.
You have to be patient with yourself.
Cherish yourself and give yourself the time to heal."
– David Elliot

Don't give up on your joy because you have a limiting belief that you can never reach it. Don't give up on yourself. You can change. You can enjoy your life more. You can heal from your wounds. Whatever you don't have now, that you want, you can have. You have to persist. You have to get back up again.

Midway through writing this, I had a crushing break up with someone I felt very much in love with. I woke up every day yearning for him, thought about him all day long, and desperately wanted to be with him and call him. Joy was the furthest thing from my heart. I could only feel sorrow.

I felt like the whole Joy Experiment was going down the crapper. Even my joyful intentions were gone. I was so sad. I didn't even feel the desire to be happy. I only wanted to "get through" the day without hurting myself. We are very used to the way we were raised. We feel comfortable with the same level of anxiety or frustration or loneliness we grew up with.

When we try to change our life, our ego reacts. It doesn't understand we are trying to make things better. It just wants stasis. This is the resistance we feel when we try to change our eating patterns or try to create a ritual of meditation. Our ego keeps us small.

Our ego is tradition. Ego says, "Your mother was depressed, you will be depressed." I must rise above that voice in my head that says "No." The ego always has a great excuse of why I can't go to a party or why I can't relax and enjoy some time off. But that ego voice is not feeding my soul. It is not loving me. It is not helping me to become the best, brightest, happiest person I can be.

My ego wants me small and safe. It wants to protect everything. It doesn't want me to raise my voice and ask for what I really want. That resistant part of me that says "Why are YOU writing a book about JOY?" is just my ego. It doesn't want me to succeed. It only cares about protecting me from getting hurt. My ego lives in fear. And if I listen to that depressed, limiting voice, I will stay exactly where I started. I won't find love. I won't succeed in my writing career. I will play it small and give up on myself. I won't finish this book. I'd probably still be calling suicide hotline on the weekends.

But I am not going to give up. And you can't either. You have to rise above the voice of defeat. If you think about it, it's probably not even your voice anyway. Doesn't it sound very familiar? Doesn't it use the same phrases that your mother used to use? Or your father? Or your grandmother? Their job was to protect you too. And they did the very best they could.

But now you are free. Now you get to create your own vision for your life and then manifest it into reality. You are no longer subject to their criticism and their limiting beliefs. It is time to rise up into your full capacity.
One step at a time.

As I edit this book, I am 93% joyful all day. I hardly recognize those negative voices because I haven't heard them in so long.

Another challenge to change is identifying with your pain. Many people, myself included (in the past!), are so identified with their story that they feel lost without it. They see themselves as a victim. When they talk to people, it is as a victim. So, once you clear all those misconceptions about yourself and realize you are 100% responsible for your life, you could find that you don't recognize yourself. You could start to talk to an old friend, realize you are falling into the old pattern and then not have anything to say. This is okay.

WELCOME TO THE FERTILE VOID
This is a place where anything can happen.
As I began to rebuild myself after the end of my last relationship, I realized I wanted to have peacefulness at my core. When I was in the relationship, peacefulness was nowhere to be found. Passion was raging, but peacefulness—not so much.

Then my healing mentor, David Elliott, told me I didn't know what love was and that I was just feeding my ego though thinking I loved this man.

So, the next part of my foundation came: love.
Love as a state of being instead of love as a feeling.
Then I added other qualities to my foundation: happiness and abundance.

Now, when I hear my victim stories rising into my throat, I stop them. I am refusing to ride that vibration any longer. I refuse to tell that story. Even if I don't have anything to say, the important thing is to be open to the newness. Something will come eventually.

Change can be uncomfortable. I just had my blood work analyzed and I found that my red blood cells are clumped together. They are dehydrated. I have fibers in my blood, which tell me that my liver is working overtime to get rid of toxins.

The solution is an entirely new diet. The foods I naturally prefer have a low pH, so my system is too acidic—which is why I keep getting sick.

Changing my eating habits is going to take time. I can't do it all at once. I need to take small steps and make them habits. My nutritionist said she can change my cravings.

But talking to her on the phone brought up all sorts of subconscious fears. Will I get enough to eat? Will I be miserable at every meal? Will I even be able to control myself enough to eat right? Will I have time to prepare organic meals? Will I have to give up meat (which I love and crave).

None of these fears are going to help me make this change. The fears are just resistance.
I need to focus on what I want: a healthy body. Then I need to take small step after small step on that path.

Thinking about all the things that are going to have to change only overwhelms me. It doesn't help me.
It is negative future fantasizing and has nothing to do with the actual process of eating right.
Who knows?
Maybe I will like the new diet?
Maybe I will like how it makes me feel and look?

Likewise, all change takes time and can be scary.
A year ago it would have been impossible to imagine being so happy everyday. But moving slowly and consciously, raising the happy bar one point at a time, I made the transition.

As I edit this (a year later), my diet has changed completely. I am mostly vegetarian and don't lean so heavily on meats and sugars. I have tons of energy and am told I look younger and more radiant. I made this transition one step at a time. I changed myself and my cravings changed naturally.

After my fair share of denial...
I won't change.
I won't change.
My cholesterol level is 220.
But I love my meat and I won't change.
Finally, I set my intention to be healthy and lower my cholesterol level.
I did the breathwork to clear the yearning and longing for meat.

I released old underlying beliefs that I needed for pleasure because I didn't have love.

I replaced it with a healthier belief, " I am lovable, I am valuable, I am loving, I am love."
I forgave myself for judging myself as needing food as a substitute for love.

And now I am basking in the natural joy, which is my birthright.

And my cholesterol level is perfect.

EXERCISE: ACKNOWLEDGE YOURSELF
What do you notice is different? Can you feel any shifts? Acknowledge every step along the way. The most minor awareness could be a huge opening. Acknowledge the time you spent learning about how to improve your life.

Acknowledge any transformations in your energy.

Acknowledge yourself for letting go of the past and stepping into the mysterious future. Acknowledge yourself for taking a chance on healing. Acknowledge any moments of being loving or compassionate to yourself. Acknowledge yourself! It feels great!

And it helps you anchor healthy patterns into your nervous system.

Stop waiting for someone else to tell you how great you are—acknowledge how great you are to yourself!!!

_____

_____

_____

_____

_____

_____

_____

_____

_____

_____

_____

_____

_____

_____

The Joy Experiment

CHAPTER TWELVE:

learning the lessons

"Out of difficulties grow miracles."

– Jean De La Bruyere

Every bad thing that happened in my life has a blessing in it. This is not to say that I want bad things to happen. Far from it. I focus on bringing in happy events and positive experiences.

God always gets this question, "Why if you exist is there pain?"

I believe his answer is: "In order for you to learn love and align with your highest self."

In every painful event in my life, I can derive a valuable lesson.

Let's look more closely:
I grew up feeling like I didn't have the love of my parents. I felt like they didn't have time for me or pay attention to me. I got whatever grades I wanted. They came to my theater shows, but they never asked me how I was doing, why I was so angry, or why I wore all black.

But because I felt like I had no parents, I developed a fierce independence. I am incredibly self-reliant. Because I didn't seek their approval, I had a lot of room to find myself, to follow my own dreams, and to dream up an outrageous personality and live it.

Through not feeling their love, I had to learn to give myself that love. I had to learn to nurture myself as a mother would and protect myself as a father would. This made me very strong.

Now I have no trouble spending hours alone accomplishing tasks because I have this early discipline of caring for myself.

In reality, the love was there. I was just unable to feel it because of my layers of isolation and they were unable to show it in the way I needed because of their own pain.

That was the final lesson I learned: the love is always there. Changing perspective like this is so empowering. I am no longer the victim of my mother's depression. I benefited from learning that I can take negative energy and turn it into positive energy. That is true learning.

Another example is when I broke up with my writing partner. I lost money, I lost security, and it looked bad on my resume. The blessing was learning my true voice, and following the guidance of the stories I am supposed to be writing. Stories that uplift people rather than fill them with fear.

Many people who have had serious life-threatening illnesses find themselves changing their lives for the first time. They grow to love themselves and the preciousness of their lives.

How can you let go of your victim story?
How can you find the blessing?
Sometimes hurts are so deep that it's hard to imagine anything good that could have come from it. If this is where you are, you probably need to heal the pain first. Don't rush the process. Feel the pain, acknowledge it, go through it,

and when you get to the other side it will be easier to see the blessing.

There is a thing called a spiritual bypass, when you bury your feelings and try to maintain the higher perspective through exercise or meditation. Spiritual bypass is almost as unhealthy as drinking away your problems. If you don't allow the feelings, you don't truly get the lesson. If you don't allow the feelings, they get buried in your body and can manifest as illnesses.

If you are ready, look at the lessons you learned and the qualities you developed from your life challenges.
One lesson I learned from what I went through was:

_____

_____

_____

_____

_____

_____

One positive quality I developed from what I went through is:

_____

_____

_____

_____

_____

_____

One blessing I am aware of is:

_____

_____

_____

_____

_____

Another positive quality I developed is:

_____

_____

_____

The Joy Experiment

finding your life purpose

"Listen to your dreams instead of your doubts."

– Sam Horn

An essential part for me to be fully joyful was finding my life purpose and fulfilling it. This inspires me throughout the day and helps me to serve others as well as myself. I feel all people have value just in being, but finding your life purpose adds a delicious passion to life. And all your gifts and creativity has power and focus guiding it.

My life has changed. I now feel guided in my actions. I feel like I know my purpose in life and I am staying on the path to follow it.

How did I uncover my life purpose?

There are four signposts that can help you uncover it.

They are:

1. What do you love to do?
2. What did you play as a child?
3. What are your strengths from your life lessons?
4. What are you naturally good at?

WHAT DO YOU LOVE TO DO?

I love to write uplifting movies. I love to write healing blogs. I love to transmute energy. I love to help others. I lose time when I am writing. I feel fully alive and I feel like I've accomplished something when I finish. Plus, I have tons of creative ideas for shows and books to write. From this, my life purpose could be a healer, a self-help novelist, or a TV and film writer/producer.

What do you love to do?

_____

_____

_____

_____

_____

WHAT DID YOU PLAY AS A CHILD?

My older brother Preston used to make a store out of a chair and a platter and sell bouncy balls and paper clips to me and my other brother. Now he's an investment banker brokering million-dollar deals. When I was a child, I liked to play Barbies and witch. My best friend and I spent hours weaving tales of intrigue, love, and betrayal. Day after day, we would create fantastic stories of heroes and villains. Love and sacrifice. And romance. A ton of romance. Ken and Barbie were very busy.

This also points in the direction of story telling, and additionally an interest in wish fulfillment and overcoming obstacles. Also, there was a magical reality aspect, so enhancing and creating reality is also part of my life purpose.

What did you play as a child?

_____

_____

_____

_____

_____

_____

WHAT ARE YOUR STRENGTHS FROM YOUR LIFE LESSONS?

I learned that I could change negative energy to positive. I learned to be independent. I learned not to judge others. I learned that I am co-creating my reality. I learned how to relax and enjoy life. These lessons give me the skills to support others in healing themselves. My past pain gives me empathy for others. I know what deep feelings of worthlessness feel like.

My sensitivity gives me knowledge of the human experience. My strength gives me the ability to deal with dark issues in my healing practice or in my writing. My courage to be joyful inspires others to be happy and to live their best life. These gifts make me an insightful storyteller or a great healer.

What are your gifts?

_____

_____

_____

_____

_____

_____

_____

The final guidepost is:

WHAT ARE YOU NATURALLY GOOD AT?

What do you get compliments on? What comes easily and naturally? I frequently get thanked for my blogs. People say that I expressed just what they were feeling, but could not find the words to say. Others told me they felt "enlightened."

I also get complements on my sense of humor and my ability to make people laugh. From this I draw the conclusion that my life purpose is inspiring others by sharing my life.

What are you good at?

_____

_____

_____

_____

_____

_____

What do your signposts point toward? For me, it is being joyful and sharing that joy. And helping people heal through writing, whether it be self-help novels, blogs, or TV and film. One's life purpose isn't necessarily about "doing." Ultimately, it should be about making the world a better place by sharing one's gifts. This should not be stressful. Your life purpose shouldn't feel like a heavy burden. If it does, you may be taking on too much. One's life purpose should feel light and fun and a joy to perform. If it feels like a "should," you might be clinging to other people's expectations of you.

When you are in alignment with your life purpose, you wake up joyful, you play at work, you have a sense of accomplishment when you finish, and you feel like you are in service to the greater good. This could look like anything: raising a family, teaching karate, being a janitor, being a famous actor, etc.

Underlying everything, I believe my life purpose is to be joyful and to radiate that joy in the world—in whatever form that takes: sharing a smile on the sidewalk, guiding a person on their life path, setting someone free to find their own way, revealing my insights in blogs, having my characters learn the blessings of their life's lessons, telling stories where people face their fears and overcome them to find happier lives.

When you put your signposts together, what seems to be your life purpose? It should feel good to reflect on it. If it doesn't, you may still have some limiting beliefs about yourself or negative judgments you need to clear.

_____

_____

_____

_____

The Joy Experiment

The Joy Experiment

going with the flow

"Everything in the universe has a purpose. Indeed, the invisible intelligence that flows through everything in a purposeful fashion is also flowing through you."

– Wayne Dyer

When you consider the universe—the millions of stars and people, the abundance of resources, the effortlessness of breathing—it seems like there is a system. Whether you believe in God or not, there is a power of creation that is undeniable. When one connects to this power, their actions become directed and guided.

It is as if you find your place in the world and everything happens effortlessly and with joy. The problem is that we build resistances and fears to life. We block our own abundance with worry and anxiety. But our natural state is relaxed and receiving all the goodness the world has to offer. All the test and triggers we experience have one purpose and that is to bring us back into alignment with ourselves and the universe. The broken record patterns will repeat until you get to a breaking point and let go.

That's when emotions crash though and you can experience forgiveness and letting go. That's when you let go of your misunderstandings and learn to trust again. We actually mend the separation of God and man through clearing the false beliefs.

When I felt alone and insecure, I also felt there was no God. I didn't believe in anything spiritual. It wasn't cool. It was only when I cleared all those misunderstandings that I had about people and life that I was able to feel and see God again.

I am not talking about the vision of a white-haired bearded man in the sky. (That's Santa Claus). I'm talking about looking at the energetic vibrations of everything and seeing the connection—the miracle of life. That's why all the myths are the same. That's why Muslims have an Allah, Jewish people have Yaweh, and Christians have God. These are all different names for the same thing: positive guiding energy.

God is the energy of love.

When I connect to this energy, everyone I meet smiles at me. Babies scrunch their noses playfully, the ideas of my scripts come pouring through me, and everything in my day falls into place with ease and grace. I want to eat the healthy salad for lunch, huge checks arrive in the mail, I finish all my work, and I still have time to meditate and take a bath.

Everything is perfect.
This is the flow.
This is the state of being that is available to all of us.

In the past, I was always rushing, always pushing, rushing through scripts, rushing through jobs, pushing people to hirer me or bribing people to date me. I would wake up with a sense of terror (usually from nightmares), and then I would take that feeling and push myself through my day.

Everything felt restricted and constricted. Everything was a "must" or a "should" or a "have to." I couldn't enjoy my day because I had this pushing energy that didn't allow me to be present. It just wanted tasks done. There was a great deal of fear behind my actions. With guys I dated, I was like a desperate rescue dog frantically doing tricks and saying "rub my belly." It's like my engine was always revved too high and it frequently caused me to burn out.

Once I began to meditate and clear the original traumas, I began to enjoy the moments of my day. I began to trust that everything would happen at its right time. I began to relax. This feels so good. It is a completely different energy than the desperate pushing energy. It is the energy of someone who can receive.

In the pushing, aggressive state there was no room to actually receive all the things I was striving for: love, understanding, a great job, a compatible life partner.

Now, I still occasionally wake up feeling that push, but then I recognize it and acknowledge it and I set it free. I consciously adjust my energy. And if I can't set it free, then it gets freed through my morning breathwork. Anxiety, anger, strain, stress, and lack of self-love all get released in a half hour of breathing.

Now, I am so grateful to be in the flow.

Here's what the flow is like:
All my needs are taken care of before I ask.
Each task is effortless and inspired.
My life is balanced with exercise, play, and meditation.
I am able to nurture myself throughout my day.
I feel vibrations and tingles in my body as I work.
I see beauty all around me in everything.
Creative projects easily download.
I deeply love and appreciate my home, my gifts, and my baby dogs.
I send blessings of light to my family and friends.
Everyone I meet is a friend.
People are kind and forgiving.
I am constantly laughing with friends.

I am aglow with radiant love.

Look for signs that you are on your path and in the flow of the universe. What feels like it is working? What might you need to change or work on? If you ask for guidance from the universe, you will receive it.

_____

_____

_____

_____

_____

_____

_____

_____

_____

_____

_____

_____

The Joy Experiment

CHAPTER FIFTEEN:

conclusions

"Birds flying high you know how I feel.
Sun in the sky you know how I feel.
Breeze drifting on by you know how I feel.
It's a new dawn. It's a new day.
It's a new life. For me. And I'm feeling good."

– Anthony Newley and Leslie Bricusse

Wow! It has been quite a journey. Quite a ride. I began feeling trepidatious and unsure of myself. Embarrassed to expose my innermost secrets. I end feeling whole. Feeling like I accept every part of me. In love with myself. In love with life.

When I began this experiment, my joy came from outside myself. Getting a job or meeting a potential partner excited me and raised my levels of joy. Now I have a steady stream of inner joy that I bring to my life. I wake up happy (which was a huge challenge previously) and I maintain an even neutral base of pleasure throughout the day so that whether I am doing dishes or going on a sweet date, I am happy.

Now, very simple things bring me joy because I am already joyful and am looking through joy-filled eyes. Seeing flowers on the street. Witnessing a kind gesture between two people. Hearing an uplifting song on the radio. Exchanging a smile with a stranger that says "I get it."

And when external things seem to go wrong, I know there is a purpose and a lesson in them. I summon my patience and have faith it will all work out in the end. I can even see the beauty in the issue—a chance to be more compassionate and attentive to myself.

I did reach a consistent 8 on the joy rating scale using my joy meters (see the final joy meter on page 202) and now —if you can believe it—joy has become slightly less important to me. Now that I know joy intimately, I have other goals, like developing my intuition, staying grounded, seeing clearly, enjoying contentedness, processing what comes forward to be processed, and being of service by making the world a better place. Once you are joyful, you can take joy into everything you do and everywhere you go.

The Joy Experiment

I know this is a process and every day I will need to make the right choices and align with my highest good. I will continue to do my breath mediation and be guided by the wisdom I receive from it.

I will continue to connect to Spirit and my Higher Self through breath meditations. I am human and I am still peeling back the layers, uncovering the truth.
But here's what I have accomplished in the process:

MY JOY INTENTIONS
It is my intention to love myself no matter my external situation. CHECK
It is my intention to feel bliss in my body. CHECK
It is my intention to be full of gratitude for the beautiful abundance in my life. CHECK
It is my intention to unconditionally accept all aspects of myself. CHECK
It is my intention to enjoy my life. CHECK
It is my intention to trust love. CHECK.
It is my intention to manifest a life partner. STILL WORKING ON THIS ONE
It is my intention to open my heart. CHECK
It is my intention to trust God to support me completely. CHECK
It is my intention to be grateful to God. CHECK
It is my intention to spread joy and excitement to others. CHECK
It is my intention to fully embrace all that life offers me. CHECK

It is my intention to face my fears and let go of them. CHECK
It is my intention to live deeply and fully. CHECK
It is my intention to love life. CHECK
It is my intention to love myself and others. CHECK
It is my intention to take a vacation. DOUBLE CHECK

I have come a long way. And I still have room to grow. I am in touch with what to focus on next. I am acknowledging my great accomplishments up to this point. Good work, Laurence!

You should acknowledge yourself too!

LIST YOUR ORIGINAL INTENTIONS AND CHECK WHAT YOU HAVE ACCOMPLISHED!
You finished this book. CHECK.
Your value is innate. CHECK.
What else? Did you raise your level of joy even 1 point?! Have you taken your first steps toward healing? Are you closer to falling in love with your life? Did you realize your life purpose? See how far you have come and acknowledge yourself!!!

_____

_____

_____

_____

_____

The Joy Experiment

_____

_____

_____

_____

_____

_____

_____

In reading this, you are on your path to enlightenment.
As you clear the traumas, you will become your own best guide to a fulfilling life.
All the answers are within you.
The breath work, self-love, and self-forgiveness will help you peel back the layers to find your inner wisdom.
Don't give up on yourself.
I believe in you.
I know you can have a happier life.
Breathe into love.
Set yourself free.
God bless you.
And God bless me.
God bless us all.

joy meter

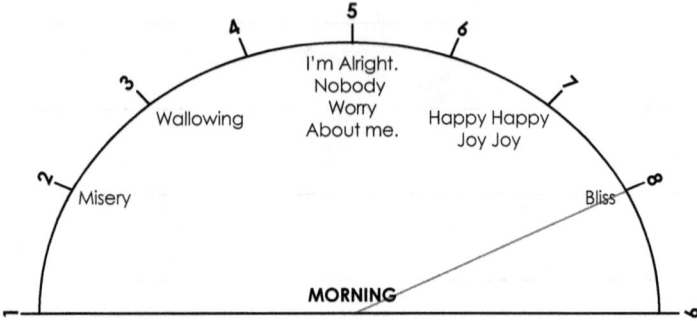

MORNING

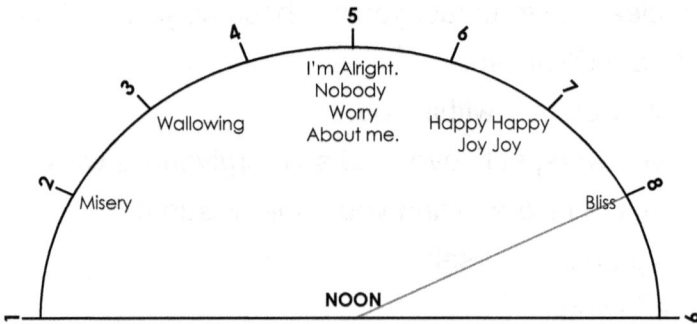

NOON

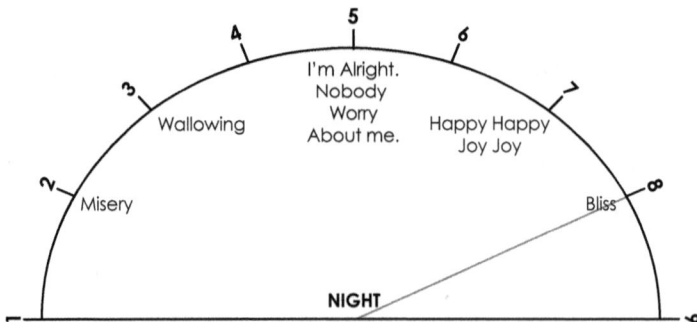

NIGHT

The Joy Experiment

acknowledgements

I have so much gratitude for all the people who inspired and encouraged this book: my father, my mother, my Step-mother, my brothers and sister, my nephews and nieces, and Qais Arefi.

Thanks also to my spiritual teachers who helped to awaken me and guide me on my path: David Elliott, Ron and Mary Hulnick, Francesca Boring, and Eileen Kenny.

I am also grateful for my spectacular editor who brought her own vast spiritual knowledge to the editing of this book, Leslie Huber. And special thanks to my energetic, unflinching cheerleaders along the way: David Paul, Katrina Rivers, Edwina Cross, and Rachel Newstat.

I have immense gratitude for my incredible web designer and friend Audrey Denson for the beautiful, joyful cover she created, as well as her loving wisdom, consistent vision, and unwavering support... "Go for the higher vibration..."

Additional thanks go out to David Michaels for his fortitude and bravery in formatting this book. And finally, a big thank you to Izzi and Dickins who are always there for me no matter what. Thank you! I love you!

www.ingramcontent.com/pod-product-compliance
Lightning Source LLC
Chambersburg PA
CBHW071431090426
42737CB00011B/1633